FROM A WONKY PATH TO AN OPEN ROAD

A SHORT BOOK ABOUT A LONG JOURNEY

Enjoy the journey!

JANEY de NORDWALL

Published by On The Road Publishing

Cover and book design by Michael Lenz

Printed by Book Printing UK

ISBN 978-1-8380930-9-9

To MAX and PAX

PHOTOS   AT THE HEAD OF SOME CHAPTERS YOU'LL SEE A SOME GRID
REFERENCES. THESE RELATE TO PHOTOS TAKEN DURING
THE ROAD TRIP THAT YOU CAN FIND IN THE FRONT AND
BACK COVER GATEFOLDS.

CHAPTERS

ONE	Who am I?
TWO	So, how do you prep for a road trip?
THREE	Where the wonky path began
FOUR	Who What Why Where When
FIVE	8th July: Pies, puddings and a wheel arch
SIX	10th July: The plague and being air-cooled
SEVEN	11th July: Cowboys and The Hard Loch Café
EIGHT	Why would a lonely person go on a solo road trip?
NINE	13th July: Rest and be thankful
TEN	Short films and red carpets
ELEVEN	14th July: Leaping salmon and rush-hour traffic
TWELVE	17th July: HebCelt heaven
THIRTEEN	21st July: Wild, wild camping in the wild, wild west
FOURTEEN	A Death, an angel and a visitation
FIFTEEN	Ashes and dust
SIXTEEN	24th July: A whisky-aided ride and a new parable
SEVENTEEN	26th July: No roads in, no roads out
EIGHTEEN	Six dinners later...
NINETEEN	27th July: I know where I am going
TWENTY	29th July: Familiar faces and hidden beaches
TWENTY-ONE	31st July: Jeremiah 29:11-13
TWENTY-TWO	3rd Aug: Are you sponsored by Bruichladdich?
TWENTY-THREE	5th Aug: Not all breakdowns are bad
TWENTY-FOUR	9th Aug: Goodbye Scotland
TWENTY-FIVE	Forty days and forty nights
EPILOGUE	The four-day bolt on
THE_END.xlsx	It's a numbers game
MY SCOTTISH ROUTE	2,471 mile round trip

ONE

Who am I?

I'm 52. Single. And have no kids.

My blood group is B positive, which is my attitude to life.

I'm also dyslexic, which I have found to be a positive disadvantage.

I was educated at an all girls' convent in Cheshire. My qualifications reached to no more than a handful of O'levels, English Language not being one of them. The nuns at school told me that I was: "*thick and lazy and would never amount to anything.*"

I have founded and run four companies. I've been a film producer, a Managing Director and a Board Director. I've won a BAFTA, been nominated for another and won numerous short film awards.

Brought up in Manchester, I now live in London and my home is my sanctuary. I have a truly amazing family and an incredible network of friends.

But I'm lonely.

I have a young British Shorthair Silver Tabby called Kenny. I own a blue 1970s VW T2 campervan called Charlie. I love photography, but I'm not a photographer and have recently started road cycling, though I'm the slowest on the road.

After three near work-related breakdowns, I left a well-paid job.

With time on my hands, some money in the bank, and in need of some therapy, I was wondering what to do next. I asked my future 80-year-old self what advice she would give me. She was pretty clear.

"*Go on a fucking road trip! Take your V-Dub, your bike, your camera and your cat. And whilst you're away write a WHO WHAT WHY WHERE WHEN of your thoughts and you'll work out it out from there..."*

I started writing this on day one of that fucking road trip! (I love the fact that I'm still swearing into my 80s.)

My writings may skip about like my dyslexic thoughts but hopefully, when linked with my meandering road trip, they'll deliver the observations of someone who finally understood WHO she was, WHERE she was going and WHAT to do next.

Kenny and Charlie are the only named references in this book, so anyone else mentioned as a 'he', 'she' or 'friend' can only wonder if it is them...

TWO

So, how do you prep for a road trip?

When my 80-year-old self told me to go on a road trip she hadn't given any hint of where I should head, or for how long I should be away, so the world was my oyster. But that was one hell of an oyster.

Europe or the UK?

Erm... UK.

Six days, six weeks or six months?

Erm... six weeks.

I chose six weeks as that would keep me on the road for 42 days. As an early teen, I loved watching the 1980s series *The Hitchhiker's Guide to the Galaxy* and, for any other Douglas Adams fans out there, you'll know that 42 is the ultimate answer to the Ultimate Question of Life, the Universe and Everything. It's also a popular pub quiz question so bank it and don't forget.

Unlike the Deep Thought computer, however, I certainly didn't have 7.5 million years to ponder so I hoped that 42 days would be just enough time to allow my mind to run wild. I realise that my expectations might have been slightly heightened to hope to find The Answer in such a short amount of time, especially as I didn't even have a clear Question in mind, but I definitely felt that an answer of some sort was heading my way, or if not, then I was heading straight for it.

In fact, I ended up being in the van for a biblical 40 days and 40 nights with a four-day bolt on that changed my life. But I'll come on to that later.

•

I'd bought Charlie the previous year with a couple of friends who were also looking to buy a camper so we decided to go in together, like a modern-day timeshare, but cooler! I own two thirds and they own the rest so all the costs are split accordingly. It works brilliantly and during spring, summer and autumn Charlie is rarely cooped up in his garage.

As I entered the world of How Not To Buy A Rust Bucket On Wheels I quickly realised how easy it was to be duped into buying a rust bucket on wheels. My level of research rose to Defcon 1 as I set out on Operation V-Dub.

After a couple of false starts and several viewings – including one particularly embarrassed looking pimped-up van complete with an exterior studded with flashing LED lights and a boot filled with mega-base speakers, who I'm sure whispered "*Help me*" as I declined to make an offer – I found Charlie. He was blue, un-pimped, right hand drive with a shiny clean engine. He was perfect. It was love at first sight.

My first boyfriend, when I was 17, had renovated his 1963 VW split screen (imaginatively called Splitty) so he was commandeered as my expert. Armed with experience and a magnet, which is one way of ensuring if a van's bodywork is original metalwork or reconstructed from chicken wire and polyfilla, he kindly came with me to check out Charlie. He crawled all over him with his magnet, which attached itself to all the right places, and came to the same conclusion as did the man from the RAC... Charlie was a good'un.

Unlike most vans, Charlie didn't have any kitchen or shelving installed so all cooking equipment would have to be brought in – camping style. The upside to having no fixtures and fittings is that the whole of the back seat turned in to one massive bed...! I could starfish on the road!

My timeshare friends and I knew that Charlie's interior needed updating so we designed bespoke storage and clever sliding wooden panels to create a mega bed over the hidden drawers below and I designed the perfectly fitting mattress cushions covered in a retro blue dotted fabric. Charlie was delighted with his makeover and was now definitely ready to hit the road in style.

•

On a phone call with another friend one morning, who was sitting in bed with her hubby, I mentioned that I was planning a road trip. He joined the conversation and immediately suggested his own dream trip of the North Coast 500. I'd never heard of it. A quick phone Google told me that it was 516 miles of the most iconic coastal routes around Scotland starting and ending at Inverness – and it sounded epic. A further laptop Google revealed multiple blogs naming it one of the 'top coastal road trips in the world', 'the ultimate road trip' and even 'Scotland's Route 66'. However, continued researches flagged sponsored websites, branded merchandise and a darker side of the locals getting pretty pissed off with all the ugly, oversized motorhomes and high-speed motorbikes ruining their roads. This was already a gringo trail! A bucket list tick off. Way too conventional for me. This needed to be *my* journey. *My* road trip. *My* route – without a branded hoodie, key ring and a #nc500.

I had also heard that the east coast roads up and around John o'Groats weren't particularly inspiring and definitely not as dramatic as the west so there could be a whole corner that could be cut out. Sorry NE Scotland, but there didn't seem much point of driving for driving's sake and I'd already seen far too many identical photos across social media of people in front the John o'Groats signpost with thumbs up in the rain.

Another friend then mentioned the HebCelt music festival in Stornaway on the Isle of Lewis. Three days of Celtic music on an Outer Hebridean isle sounded heavenly but almost too far out of reach. It sounded like Outer Mongolia to me, somewhere so glamorously remote that no one could even get there. Could I even take a campervan and a cat...? But it really struck a Celtic chord with me so I knew, by hook or by crook, I would have to find a way of getting to that exotic Isle. We looked it up and, as if luck would have it, it was taking place mid-July which worked out to be 10 days after my departure date. Oooh... I could make this work!

●

As a producer, I knew that a successful event needed great planning and every great producer knows that you need a spreadsheet to plan. And I really love a spreadsheet. Like *really* love them. I love them so much I even designed the interior of Charlie on one, and the Mondrian-style shelving in my home and even recreated a Bridget Riley on Excel! But no, for the first time I was going to go off grid with no plan, no spreadsheet. It felt right. It felt liberating. It felt terrifying! What the hell was I thinking? How can anything happen if it's not in a box, data sorted with formulas and colour coded with a key? But an analogue world of adventure was calling so I deleted RoadTrip2019.xlsx and got out my little red notepad and pencil.

In preparation for the road trip, there were several things on my list but I decided that my number one consideration was my traveling companion. Cats aren't known for their love of camping so would Kenny be a happy camper...?

Kenny is a beautiful eighteen-month-old British Shorthair Silver Tabby who lives indoors in my East End flat for fear of being stolen and sold for crack. Even though I keep my front door open Kenny happily sits on the mat looking out. The great outdoors seems very low on his adventure scale. His main sources of entertainment include looking out of the window at the dealers below, careering up and down the spiral staircase at great speed and chasing flies. I pimped-up his scratch post with feathers and bells and it now looks like a weird hippy dreamcatcher thing but he loves it and scratches the b'jesus out of it rendering my furniture unscathed. Like a familiar, he follows me from room to room.

He's an absolute joy and the perfect companion. It has to be said that I am a very happy middle-aged cat lady that hopefully doesn't smell of *Eau de Chat* just yet.

So, I needed a pre-road trip test to make sure that Kenny would be happy living in a van, whilst also ensuring that Charlie's new interior remained untouched by his sharp, shiny claws.

Amazingly, I found an off-grid campsite only 45 minutes out of London. It was a 250-acre chestnut wood hidden away in the middle of Kent with organic non-flushing toilets, hot showers, fire pits and chickens running around offering their eggs for breakfast. Each camping space was completely surrounded by trees so you felt like you were alone in the wilderness. It was cat friendly, perfect for the test and steeped in history. William the Conqueror had gifted the then deer park to his half-brother Odo and then, during WWII, it had been commandeered by the army as a Pre-Officer Training Camp. As you wander through the wild woods you can still find and follow the remains of the trenches they dug out.

So I booked two nights for me, Kenny, my friend and her two cats with whom she regularly travels. Her cats are also flat cats but are seasoned travellers in her campervan and are used to being on the end of a harness and lead. After parking up, opening the side door, building a fire and eating dinner in the great outdoors we watched with glee when Kenny finally tiptoed out of the van for the very first time. Sporting his new purple harness and lead he seemed to enjoy the sensation of woodland under his urban paws. Even though he Houdinied out of his little purple harness within an hour, he amazingly kept close to the van and didn't bolt. We replaced his little harness with a larger Houdini-proof leopard print version which I was happier with but I'm not so sure he agreed with the mixing of animal prints.

As with any cat, Kenny's facial expression never gives much away. *"What on earth are you doing?"* and *"This is the most exciting day of my life!"* look exactly the same (as an example, I refer you back to the front cover... which caption would you use?). I chose to read his Botoxed face as *"thoroughly excited"* at the prospect of a Scottish adventure. Although my fingers, toes, legs and eyes were all crossed in the hope that I had read him right, I made a pact with myself that if Kenny showed any signs of stress during the journey I would bring him home.

•

I then had to face the fact that Charlie, handsome though he was, at 49 years old would inevitably break down along the way. Now, this may sound like a pessimistic way to start a journey of a lifetime, but one thing that my producing years have taught me is to solve a problem before it arises. Having a Plan B & C up my sleeve has always served me well and this was definitely going to be a *when* not an *if*. But what is an adventure without a breakdown, be it mechanical or emotional, and, as I had already banked a few emotional ones, I was holding out for the former.

I called my effervescent mechanic who generously gave me a two-hour lesson on air-cooled engines and how to change a tyre. The good thing about these old engines is that you can see every component so it makes it a lot easier to pinpoint the problem in order to resolve it. I videoed him as he talked me through the parts of the engine that I should keep my eye on.

"So, Janey, if the van ever breaks down then it's going to be down to two things: fuel or electrics," he explained.

Well that sounded easy enough and we began to comb through the engine paying extra attention to the fuel pipe, oil, the coil, spark plugs, and so on. I was in heaven. He also suggested I collated an 'on the road box of tricks' including a spare fan belt, throttle cable, clutch cable, spark plugs, set of bulbs, electrical cables and cable ties.

He also lent me a few tools for the journey including his breaker bar, which is a long, heavy steel rod to lever the nuts off the wheel in the event of a puncture. He said that if I ever got into trouble with an axe-wielding kilt-wearing maniac then it was also known as an 'attitude adjuster'. He ended our session by saying, *"If you ever get into trouble then call me. Anytime... anywhere!"* With all of the above, I definitely felt safer and more confident about my potential mechanical breakdowns or maniac encounters.

•

The next stage was to work out what on earth to pack and how to fit it all in a small van, allowing me the space to live and Kenny the chance to scamper. I've never been one for travelling light as I believe it to be prudent to have options for all occasions, but I knew that space would be of the essence and therefore essential items only would make it into the van.

I broke it down into the following components: Eating - Cooking - Kit - Anti-Midge Ingredients - Kenny's Stuff - My Stuff - Tech.

I've always loved packing and this goes back to when I was a child. Our family holidays would be either to London, Cornwall or Scotland which meant five- or six-hour drives from Manchester to each destination in my grandfather's Ford Zodiac. Even then I looked forward to the long drive and used to have a tiny blue suitcase about 10"x6" with a shiny red handle that would sit in the back of the car with me. For about a week before setting off, I would plan and pack fun things for my journey. These would include my Snoopy diary, a puzzle, a packet of crisps, a chocolate bar, a toy of some sort, a selection of Whimsies, a notepad and coloured pencils etc, but the key component was not *what* I packed but *how* they were packed as they all had to fit together with no gaps. If there was a gap then I would either have to repack in a different order, eat the chocolate bar, remove a Whimsy or two or fill the gap with another Whimsy or two or add something I didn't actually need. This insight alone will probably explain a lot about my personality, control issues and the need for everything to be *just so*. I still do the same when I unpack my food shopping from the trolley to the moving belt in a supermarket, though I now resist the urge to eat before buying or fill the gaps with unwanted goods.

It was clear to me that I had to follow similar principles for packing Charlie as I had five drawers, a long narrow cupboard above the back seat and a big boot to fill. I could picture the Excel spreadsheet forming in my head but once again I resisted. This was going to be fun without computer wizardry and it took me two weeks to get it right!

Drawer #1 – Eating

Apart from capers I eat everything and I'm as healthy as I can be when I'm out and about but I'm not a happy cook in the kitchen when home alone. I find it especially hard to motivate myself to cook for one and many a time I have settled down after a hard day's work to a packet of Twiglets and a crumpet, washed down with a glass of wine. No guilt. But I really wanted to eat well whilst away on my travels.

A dear friend of mine, concerned about my Twiglet habit, felt that I would need more fresh produce in me and told me how easy it was to sprout beans. *"Great idea! I'll do that!"* I had no idea what she was talking about. Luckily, a couple of days before I left, we arranged to meet and she talked me through how to sprout mung beans, buck wheat, chickpeas and alfalfa in recycled takeaway containers. She brought me a selection of these dried goods complete with written instructions and a selection of other magical essentials to pep up my dinners: roasted seeds and nuts, a balsamic spray, soy sauce, honey and pul biber. She said all I needed was some fresh Scottish salmon and I could prepare a meal fit for a queen. I had to trust her on that one!

Drawer #2 – Cooking

What to cook on was the next question. Now, I do like a bit of kit so I decided to cover all bases when it came to cooking up. If the campsite had an electrical hook up then my new double hob would be perfect. In the absence of electricity, then gas would take over and my new two ring burner with hot plate and griddle would be the star attraction. And if all else failed, my trusty foldaway fire pit would double as a BBQ. Therefore, a 230V lead, a large 3kg gas cylinder and a box of matches were also packed.

Drawer #3 – Kit

In fact, you can't have enough kit and creature comforts when it comes to camping, so a whistling kettle that matched the colour of Charlie was a given, a very cool roll up knife and bamboo utensil kit was purchased, a Swiss Army knife and a whittling knife (you never know when you might need to whittle something), a stackable set of pots, pans and handles, a mug with a matching blue VW campervan on it for morning cuppas, all topped off with my parents' bright orange melamine crockery set from the '70s and individual sets of camping cutlery. My mini mobile kitchen was complete.

Drawer #4 – Anti-Midge Ingredients

One thing I had been warned about in every blog I had read was the blight of midges. They are the bane of any Scottish holiday and love to hang out near rivers and form mists around people's heads. In fact their collective noun is a bite, which says it all. My anti-midge drawer contained everything I needed to keep these blighters at bay including a family jar of Marmite (yes, midges are haters), citronella incense sticks, citronella candles, wrist and ankle bands, my Vitamin B tablets which I had been taking for a month and a black mosquito net that covered my head and shoulders.

However, my main line of defence was a body spray from Avon, yes, *"Ding dong, Avon calling!"*, called Skin So Soft. They had adopted the Ronseal approach to naming their product as it did indeed make your skin ever so soft. However, inadvertently they had created a product that also repelled mosquitos and midges so effectively that the Army and Navy now buy it by the tonne for their soldiers and sailors. It's good to know that our fighting forces are hard on the inside, soft on the outside and totally bite free.

Drawer #5 – Kenny's stuff

For a little fella, Kenny took up quite a lot of space. Not just one drawer full of his food, a wardrobe of harnesses, leads and toys but I had his bed on the back seat and his covered litter tray in the boot. To be honest, I could have got away without his bed as he ended up finding one particular spot in the van to sleep when we were driving. It was a space that I didn't even know existed – a three-inch gap underneath the passenger seat around which he had to contort himself to get into, but once he was there he would be content and asleep for hours.

2 x Muji PP drawers – My Stuff

For some reason I had imagined myself looking rather glamorous whilst on the road so I packed some lovely floaty, pretty things. The kind of things I would have worn in Cannes. Obviously, none of these items were even unpacked as I pretty much wore the same four pieces of clothing which were washed, dried and worn on repeat. Cut-off jeans, full length jeans, t-shirt, fleece.

As a cyclist, I did of course have a drawer dedicated to Lycra – a collection that's also taking over my drawers at home at an alarming rate. I believe I have become what they refer to as a MAFIL: a Middle Aged Female In Lycra.

Long cupboard above the back seat – Tech

I knew that music would play a major role in my travels so I'd downloaded some mega Spotify playlists for different moods and occasions. Dark and moody orchestral to match the cinematic vistas whilst driving and motivational tunes for when I would be cycling up and down hills. I'd also found a portable speaker that fitted perfectly into one of the water carriers on my bike so I could ride and sing. Things that fit perfectly make my heart sing!

I bought strings of battery-powered fairy lights and solar-powered flickering candles to illuminate Charlie at night and turn him into the cosiest little playhouse imaginable. What is it about fairy lights? Twinkly lights can so easily transform a cold van into a cosy little home.

The long cupboard was also the perfect secret storage place for my laptop, camera and lenses.

•

So, finally, after a couple of weeks, everything was bought, packed and Operation Blue Suitcase was complete. I was delighted with the contents and configuration of my drawers.

I thought I was ready to tick everything off my list when I found out that anyone planning on jumping on ferries to different Isles should buy all ferry tickets in advance. Really? That meant I'd need to know where I was going! That kinda crushed my idea of being a free-spirited spontaneous adventurer and a spreadsheet of ferry times and locations almost pulled into focus. CalMac run the ferries in Scotland and I almost drowned looking at the number of hopscotch ferry options on their website. 32 in all. The man on the phone assured me that as long as I had a ticket for each ferry of choice then I could change the dates and times at any point. Now we've all experienced frustrating customer service call-centres so this ease of change sounded a bit too good to be true but I just hoped he meant it. Our conversation ended with me becoming the proud owner of three hopscotch journeys across the Isles of Lewis, Harris, Skye and Mull involving seven ferries in all. I did, indeed, put their customer service to the test on all occasions by changing every date and every time of every ferry but, credit where credit's due, their customer service and efficiency were flawless. Go CalMac!

Finally, the last piece of the puzzle. I'd thought long and hard about what my first song of the trip should be. Something uplifting to give me courage? A power ballad to belt out? A moody orchestral number to make me focus? In the end, I opted for the disc I'd keep on my Desert Island. Favourite song, favourite band, perfect lyrics. *Now you're at the wheel / Tell me how, how does it feel? / So good to have equalised / To lift up the lids of your eyes...*

•

D-day had arrived. Charlie was packed to perfection, sans gaps, and Kenny was in position avec harness and lead. I had my traditional snacks to hand to begin a long drive – a bar of Dairy Milk, a packet of Walkers cheese and onion crisps and a can of Red Bull. It was time to go. Key in the ignition. Gulp?! I suddenly realised that I had been so distracted by planning and packing the practicals that I hadn't even considered how I would actually feel now I *was* at the wheel.

Key out of the ignition. Oh God, I think I'm terrified. Out on the road, on my own, with a cat, with no sense of direction?! And that's me without the sense of direction, not Kenny. Was this just an eccentric gesture to entertain my friends, or was this the right way to find my equilibrium? Either way, it was a leap into the unknown.

I took a long breath and drummed my fingers on Charlie's bus-like steering wheel. I knew that my instincts had always served me well and, when I'd listened to them, they had always taken me down the right path, however wonky. And today? Now? Tell me! My instincts were telling me to throw caution to the wind and to leap with faith. It *was* the right thing to do. So, with eyelids lifted, I leapt. Key back in the ignition.

I turned the key and Charlie purred into action. But then, my neighbour, who I'd only spoken to twice before and who had been watching me pack for the last couple of hours with intrigue, knocked on my window. With an old polaroid camera in her hand, she asked if she could take a picture of the three of us – me, Kenny and Charlie. How sweet! So I jumped out, took Kenny off his lead and held onto him for dear life hoping he wouldn't jump off, run away and ruin the whole trip (I hadn't prepared a Plan B for that one) and we all posed proudly for her. She then gave me the tiny polaroid to keep on my dashboard as a good luck charm. As I drove out of the courtyard, she waved me off at the gates with a white hanky as I sang *Waterfall* by The Stone Roses loud and proud.

It was a perfectly quirky way for my journey to begin.

THREE

Where the wonky path began

Before I embark on my journey, or even start to air the revelations that revealed themselves during my 2,471-mile drive, I thought I'd share some key moments in my life where my decisions, however unusual or unconventional, have led me to this life-affirming, life-changing road trip. I call these my wonky paths as I prefer these to the straight 'n' narrow ones.

I'd always liked Steve Jobs' Stanford Commencement speech about joining the dots: *"You can't connect the dots looking forward; you can only connect them looking backwards. So, you have to trust that the dots will somehow connect in your future. You have to trust in something – your gut, destiny, life, karma, whatever."*

From shy to confident, from drifter to driven, looking back at my dots I can now see how their connection took me to the open road and beyond. I've tended to make choices that nestle between my comfort zone and panic zone. It's only there that real excitement, nerves and fear collide and it's only there that magic can happen. Having said that though, nothing dramatically 'magical' has happened in my life and I haven't 'made it' in the traditional sense, but, for me, I've pushed some boundaries and I'm proud to say that I've achieved more than I ever imagined and have no regrets. I reckon that's magical enough.

Anyway, the idea of 'making it' is totally subjective and you don't need to have climbed to the pinnacle of your career ladder, banked millions or brushed with fame to have made it, though social media would disagree. Nor do you need to have sailed the oceans solo or walked around the world barefooted raising money for charity to feel a sense of achievement. Most of us are pretty normal and fight our own fight for happiness and contentment in our own courageous way.

•

I started off as a very small, painfully shy child and showed no talent for anything early on. I see parents now being obsessed, and prematurely proud, that their children are showing early signs of being a doctor or an artist. I don't believe that a child knows what they want to be at an early age, and it's certainly not a sign of things to come if they like the sight of blood or can paint with their feet. There's nothing wrong with being a slow developer. I was a snail.

In comparison, my older sister was a rising star and from the age of four upwards she could converse confidently with anyone and held an impressive vocabulary of multi-syllabled words. Whilst she chatted away, I was more than happy to hide in her shadow for many years. To be honest, life in the shadows was pretty easy. Just watching and observing and taking it all in, banking it for a later date. But I was a very well spoken, smiley young girl and everyone thought I was rather sweet and those traits alone have opened many doors and got me a long way.

I was bullied at my first primary school, loved my second one and was then totally bewildered by my senior school. When I say bullied, I mean by the teachers too. At five years old I was slapped so many times on one day that I had a teacher-sized hand bruise on my tiny little thigh. Upon seeing the bruise at the end of the day my Kindergarten teacher covered it up with one of those extra sticky fabric plasters and told me not to tell my parents. It was one of those plasters that took about an hour to peel off, and I peeled all seven inches off alone in the bathroom, crying, hoping my parents wouldn't see the bruise.

She did this because I didn't know the answer to a fun puzzle at the end of a reading book. "*What's brown and hairy and full of milk?*"

"*Cow!*" was my first enthusiastic but incorrect answer.

From then on, every incorrect answer that followed received a sharp slap on my leg. However many slaps I received, and breaks she didn't allow me to take, I couldn't render the answer of something I hadn't even heard of. By the afternoon break, seeing me crying and rubbing my leg, my little friend cupped her hand and covertly whispered the answer in my ear. Even then I knew I had to offer up a couple of wrong ones first, and succumb to extra slaps, for fear of the teacher realising I had been helped. Finally the word "*Coconut*" was uttered. As she placed the plaster the length of my thigh she said "*Well, I don't know why you didn't say that in the first place,*" and sent me back to my seat. What a great learning experience. The lesson being... well, I still don't know. Tell your kids about coconuts early in life in case they come across a sadistic teacher?

On to senior school and the nuns at the convent didn't hit but they just didn't care. They taught by rote and didn't have any God given skills to inspire. One of the big things that always confused me during my school days, and definitely set me apart from everyone else, was how all my classmates seemed to be able to follow and understand the lessons and then had the ability to revise, remember and then it write it all down in an exam. And how come they were all able to read aloud? The only time I prayed was in English as I tried to shrink into oblivion behind an open book hoping that I was never asked to read aloud and be humiliated in front of my friends. I just couldn't do it. The words on a line kept moving around, and my eyes would dart around the page trying to make sense of it all, and then all the words would come out in the wrong order.

Dyslexia wasn't recognised in the '80s and was known as the Lazy Disease. To be repeatedly reminded by the nuns that I was thick and lazy only made me shrink into the shadows even more and try even less.

Although totally unrelated, it's interesting how a similar feeling would return as an adult every four weeks in the form of PMT. That feeling of 'why does everyone else know how to do it? Why don't I fit in? Why can't I do it?' Though I'm still not sure what 'it' is! 'It' probably isn't anything at all. A misconception of how one should be or just a hormonal imbalance, but either way, not being able to do, have or get 'it' has definitely played a leading role in making me feel like a loner.

To the dismay of my parents, I left my expensive fee-paying all girls convent with just three O'levels. I got a U (unclassified) in English Language, my own language for God's sake! My school careers adviser was a great help and suggested that I should work in a library. I'm pretty sure a dyslexic librarian who hated reading wouldn't have lasted long, but thanks for the advice Sister.

I retook my O'levels at the local tech in Stockport where I promptly found boys, started smoking, developed a broad Stockport accent and decided to shave my hair off and become a psychobilly. Ah, those heady days! For such strict parents my Mum and Dad were remarkably patient as I came back from clubs midweek with footprints on my face from wrecking in a mosh pit at King Kurt gigs.

I loved college as I was always at the top of my class, which was more of a reflection of the inabilities of my classmates rather than my new found intelligence, and left with four more O'levels, a great quiff but still no passion for anything nor drive to start a career. The furthest I got to securing a job was to skim the pages of the jobs section in the Manchester Evening News on a Tuesday.

Without gainful employment, and still living at home, my Dad tirelessly suggested that I should get my typing skills. In those days you had to go to typing college and sit in front of a huge keyboard projected on a wall. With headphones on, a stern voice would call out random letters at an ever-increasing speed. The letters on the wall would light up and you had to punch them out, with the correct finger, without looking down, on a letter-less keyboard. Not wanting to give in to the stereotype of becoming a female typist, I pooh-poohed the idea on every occasion to the ever-increasing sighs of my Dad.

And then success. My first job didn't require typing skills, in fact it didn't require any skills at all. It was in a shop that sold nothing of consequence.

Granada Studios Tour was Manchester's only tourist attraction that allowed visitors to go behind the scenes of famous television sets like Coronation Street and Sherlock Holmes. It felt very much like an exceedingly poor and unwanted relation of an all-singing all-dancing American studio tour, but with no personality and instantly forgettable.

I was deployed to a shop called Maddison's selling things like oversized Bet Lynch earrings and Newton & Ridley beer mats with piped Simon & Garfunkel's *Cecilia* on a loop all day. If this wasn't penance for being allegedly lazy at school, I don't know what was.

With no obvious link to any Granada television shows, visitors entered the tour at a New York street scene complete with cop cars and yellow cabs adorned with out of work actors dressed as cops and cabbies. The excited visitors were then greeted by a mascot – another out of work actor dressed up as a child with an oversized head, called OB, which stood for Outside Broadcast, which also didn't make any sense as the whole tour was based on studio-based programmes. Guests were then taken on guided group tours down the real Coronation Street, the set of Baker Street and a studio version of the Houses of Commons. A fun-packed hour.

I was soon promoted from earrings and beer mats to work in *Telestars* where lucky visitors could pay an extra £10 to be super-imposed into the Rovers Return. They entered a blue Chroma Key room, with a blue Chroma Key bar with five scripted lines on the wall with a light next to each one. Upon illumination, they would awkwardly read out a line not quite knowing where to look, who had asked them a question or even what the conversation was about.

After their scene was over, they were then presented with a VHS of themselves 'inside' the Rovers 'chatting' with Mike Baldwin and Betty Turpin about the price of houses on the street whilst sipping an invisible pint of Newton & Ridley. One of the worst uses of technology I had ever seen. One visitor told me that it was the best experience of her life. I feared for what had come before.

But it was at Granada Studios Tour that I met a new friend who started on the same day, and together we stacked shelves at Maddison's. She was fresh out of Manchester Poly with a degree in Sociology and Politics and told me that she was looking for a job in 'the media' hence working at Granada Studios Tour to get a foot in the door. I couldn't quite work out which door at GST would actually lead anywhere though... the EXIT seemed the best door in the house. She would trawl through the Media Section of The Guardian every Monday looking for jobs.

I genuinely asked her *"What's the media?"* She gave me a verbal Dummies Guide on The Media and then went on to say she was going to go to typing school to increase her chances of working in 'the media'. I decided to follow in her footsteps as it all sounded rather exciting, especially as the entry level was on reception so my lack of qualifications didn't seem to matter at all. My Dad was delighted to pay for me to finally go to typing school. Money well spent, thanks Dad. He was right, as ever.

We both landed our first jobs on reception in a post-production facility called Editz. With a Z. It was the late '80s. However, I quickly realised that I was a dreadful receptionist as I couldn't remember anyone's name and kept putting people through to the wrong edit suite. I also found the post-production process rather dull. The bit before the edit sounded far more interesting so I decided that production was my new vocation. But I didn't actually know anything about production and therefore had no idea how to get in but that didn't seem to put me off, I was determined to work in production. I realise now that this was my first turn onto my first wonky path.

I found out that most people who worked in production were freelance and that the best way to start out would be as a Production Assistant or Researcher. *"What's freelance?"* I thought. *"Oh God, what's a Production Assistant or Researcher?"* Remember there was no internet then, so a quick Wiki or a rummage around Google wasn't an option.

At that time, the Conservative government had launched the Enterprise Allowance Scheme – a controversial initiative supporting entrepreneurialism by encouraging people to sign off the dole and set up their own companies. One in six start-ups failed but amongst the clever ones were the likes of Alan McGee of Creation Records, Tracey Emin, Superdry and Viz Magazine. And then there was me. Equipped with no further knowledge on production, nor the skills required, I attended a compulsory one-day course on How To Run Your Own Company and promptly became a Freelance Production Assistant & Researcher. I then received my guaranteed £40/week and got my rent paid whilst I worked out what the hell I was meant to do with this new exciting title and freshly printed business cards.

Ignorance was indeed bliss and the key to launching my blissful freelance career was to say "*YES*" to everything and to enjoy every role that deviated from my title on my business card. Experience didn't seem to matter, so I kept smiling and never gave away that I was making it up as I went along. A handful of my early freelance roles still make me smile today...

My first ever job was as a carpenter, aka a chippie, building a set for Revlon where Take That performed one of their first ever live dance routines as a group. The stage we built looked great but the five young lads jumping around the stage wearing different shades of all-in-one Lycra bodysuits miming to a song wasn't the most impressive performance I had seen. Thank goodness for them I wasn't a talent scout. In fairness, thank God for me I wasn't one either as I couldn't have spotted a multi-million-pound global phenomenon even if it had danced in front of me in Lycra.

I then stumbled into a production admin role for a light entertainment show called *Celebrity Chefs* though I questioned the use of the word 'celebrity' in the title on many occasions. My role was the lowest on the production ladder so I eagerly watched everyone at work wondering if I could ever be good enough to do their jobs. We spent seven weeks filming around Wales with a chef no one knew. We had to follow unsuspecting shoppers around a supermarket until we could persuade one of them to allow our unknown chef, and the camera crew, to come back to their kitchen that day so that our 'celebrity' could cook up something from their basket. The emphasis was very much on 'light' when it came to entertainment value. By the end of filming I'd learnt nothing about cooking but had realised that I did indeed have the production skills required to climb the ladder. So up I went.

When a London production company was looking to shoot in the North they somehow found me and asked me to Location Manage for D:Ream's *Party Up The World*. We filmed in the enormous 250-foot satellite dish at Jodrell Bank and were given permission to upturn the dish to allow the band and about 30 dancers to strut their stuff. I'm not sure I can take total credit for securing that location as strings had definitely been pulled by Dr Brian Cox, the band's keyboard player and particle-physicist. Incidentally, Jodrell Bank, was recently declared a UNESCO World Heritage Site so I doubt anyone will be partying up their world in that dish again.

Unit Manager on Simply Red's *Fairground* was another fun one, but not for the fainthearted. Part of the promo took place on a big dipper so we hired The Big One at Blackpool Pleasure Beach for the night. We needed to shoot multiple takes of the band on the ride but sadly didn't have the budget for enough extras. My newfound negotiation skills came into play as I cajoled any available crew member into filling the empty seats on every take. And remember, this was *multiple* takes. I'm not sure if they ever forgave me as they hurtled around 5,497 feet of track with a G-force of 3.5 on repeat. Sick bags in hand.

Freelancing was definitely fun for a few years, and I certainly honed my skills at being flexible and up for anything, and didn't mind the uncertainty of job security which goes hand in hand in the freelance world. I remember talking to a friend who worked in HR where her groundhog weekly, daily, hourly schedule was set in stone. From the minute her alarm went off she knew what time she'd be out of the shower, when her hair dryer would burst into life, which carriage and seat to choose on her commuter train in and when to crack open the Belvita's for her first morning break, and so on. It sounded positively dystopian and the horror must have been reflected on my face. She asked me about mine. I told her that every day was different and I'd set a new time on my alarm the night before. I never knew what I might be doing on any given day and that I had no idea what I'd be working on in a week's time. I've never seen anyone (apart from the crew on the *Fairground* promo) look quite so sick! Each to their own I guess.

But then an opportunity for a full-time role as the Co-ordinator in a small production company came along. They shot television commercials on celluloid, just like the movies. This sounded very exciting so I waved a fond farewell to my free-spirited video-based freelance life and said a cheery hello to my first PAYE pay-slip in the film world. This was also the first time I had aspirations higher than just getting the next frivolous production role. I could see this job leading towards the dream job that I had buried for a while...

•

When I was 13, I remember watching a documentary, *The Making Of Indiana Jones and The Temple of Doom*, while munching on Christmas dinner leftovers. As they took us behind the scenes, I couldn't quite believe that these people, the ones behind the camera, did such exciting jobs. They were actually being paid to throw water on an elephant because the elephant was wet in the previous scene, or to make little models of the set and shoot this in stop-frame animation to match the live action, or gather hundreds of extras together to create a fight scene, or optically create special effects on film... Extraordinary! Why were we not told about these jobs at school? That would have certainly kicked my so-called lazy arse into touch. But my 'thick and lazy' label given to me by the nuns had stuck and this 13-year-old girl had no confidence or vision so never allowed this dream to develop. I just couldn't imagine a reality where, one day, one of those people behind the scenes of a movie could be me.

Then, in my early twenties, I was given a book called *A Day In The Life Of Hollywood*. A large photographic book made up of pictures all taken on one single day in Hollywood. Another behind-the-scenes insight from casting calls to seeing inside make-up movie trailers, from script read-throughs to location recces. It looked thrilling. But one image stood out like a beacon. A huge empty studio with a small shaft of light coming through the loading doors. A woman sitting alone at a make-shift desk made from an upturned wooden crate, with her brick-like mobile phone in hand. For me, that was the most inspiring, exciting image I had ever seen. (She's on page 64 if you ever find the book!) You can keep your red carpets and the glamour of acting, I realised then that she was exactly who I wanted to be. I remember thinking. *"If that's where it all begins, I want to be the one who makes it happen."*

•

During my first week of my new full-time job, I was asked to schedule the script for the 1996 Manchester Olympic Games Bid film. I had no idea how to do this and there was no one to ask. I realise now that I have always come across a lot more confident on the outside than I have ever felt on the inside, as inside I could feel myself shrinking back into the schoolgirl that couldn't read aloud. I chose to approach this the only way I knew how. Logically...

This was, of course, pre-computers and the internet so, with typewriter, Tippex, reams of paper, phone book, pencil, ruler and an A to Z of Manchester in hand I began. Waves of nausea would come and go at the thought of making a mistake and being humiliated in the production office but I was determined to make this work. Mistakes were not an option. Even though I had never even seen a production schedule I could see exactly what it should look like so I dived in.

First, with pencil and ruler, I created a grid on paper (my first offline Excel spreadsheet) and wound it into the typewriter. The script had a number of locations so I'd put them in column one. Each location needed a point of contact that went into column two with their telephone numbers that I'd found in the phone book. The locations were spread all over Manchester which meant removing the paper from the typewriter, marking up the locations, grouping them in geographical order and re-typing the spreadsheet. Some locations were internal shots and some were exterior shots so two new columns for that. I was really enjoying this process until I realised that I needed to speak to all the contacts on the phone! I hid in another room away from everyone to make every call.

After a couple of days, the director looked over my shoulder and asked which script breakdown method I had been taught at film school. *Film school...?* Eek! My heart stopped as I prepared to be found out and marched out of the office. I nervously admitted that I hadn't been to film school to which he replied *"Oh well, whatever you're doing looks great. Well done."* Manchester didn't win the bid in 1996 but I sat another inch taller and gained another inch of confidence. Ironically, it was this very man who also broke my professional confidence and spirit ten years later.

I stayed at this production company for several years. I worked hard, asked a lot of questions, listened and thoroughly enjoyed the vertical learning curve of production, but after a while there were several things that made me feel uncomfortable. Watching the producer hammer the crew down on unnecessary deals to then show me pictures of his new kitchen and new car didn't sit right with me. But my biggest bugbear was being told I was *"not allowed to speak in meetings."*

By the time I'd risen to Assistant Producer, I knew I needed to spread my wings, make my own decisions, use my voice and be heard. I made a radical decision to leave production and try out the advertising agency side instead. I freelanced as a TV Producer running the television department of a small but fun agency. After about six months, my wonky path took a hard right when the agency fell out with one of their biggest clients. The client then came directly to me asking if I would produce their film work.

"*Are you offering me a full-time job?*" I asked them.

"*No, not really. Can't you produce our films as a freelancer?*" they replied.

"*No, not really! I could only handle your productions and budgets either as an employee or as a limited company,*" I explained.

"*Then why don't you set up a company?*" they suggested.

Left with no other immediate option I rather quickly said: "*Oh, OK.*"

And as simply as that, I suddenly leapfrogged to a Producer & Managing Director. "*Good Lord, what on earth does a Managing Director do?*" I thought, as my Dad explained the fiduciary duties of a company director in layman's terms and I registered Silver Films Limited with Companies House.

I'm 28 years old at this point.

With Silver Films launched, I immediately found a niche in the computer games industry with that aforementioned client producing their television and cinema commercials, game promos and live events and was soon put on a monthly retainer.

I was given a selection of consoles and piles of games and I'd get home from work and have to play for hours. I'd skip dinner and loo breaks to perfect Lara Croft backflipping gracefully into speed boats to navigate the canals of Venice or get Abe to successfully sneak past the Mudokons to save his fellow slaves from Oddworld. This was all necessary research as I needed to know the games inside out. I needed to understand the characters, the language and their motivations in order to make films and help launch the games. Research at its best. I was being paid to play games! Where was the O'level for that?

As an outcome, I became a 'girl gamer' and one of a handful of production companies in the UK to service the games industry. In those days girl gamers were rare creatures and jokes about developing a virtual ironing game for girls were still deemed funny around the board room.

Out of the blue, I received a phone call from a production company in Scotland who were developing a new TV programme aimed at gamers. They were looking for a female co-host who could talk convincingly about games but also encourage more girls to join in the frenzy. They were calling to invite me up for a screen test to which, without hesitation, I declined. I knew my dyslexia prevented me from reading aloud so I wouldn't have been able to read the autocue. I politely told them that my place was behind the camera rather than in front of. That was definitely a sliding doors moment.

It was also a moment of realising I wanted more...

FOUR

Who What Why Where When

As you can imagine, the gaming world back then was a lot of fun and it didn't really feel like work. By the age of 32, I had proved to myself that I could make things happen, run a company and turn a profit and produce short form promos and commercials. I was really starting to see myself as that woman in the huge studio sitting on upturned crate. I even had a Nokia 101 mobile phone!

But it was now time to evolve. I wanted to tell stories instead of soundbites and wanted to work with real actors rather than animated games characters. I needed to challenge my instincts and emerge as a different kind of producer – a film producer. I was curious to find out if I could go the distance, as in discover a script, raise the finance, produce a film and take it to market. I even wondered if Hollywood might be calling... which takes me back to a Producer I once worked with. Every time the phone rang in the production office he'd say "*It's either Hollywood or Cricklewood.*" For some reason it still makes me laugh now! It's not even that funny!

I was at home one afternoon chatting to my parents and told them about my new movie ambitions. Mum was a 'should-have-been-artist' if only her strict aunt who was paying for her education had been less Victorian, more open-minded and not insisted on her becoming a secretary; and Dad was a Management Consultant at ICI.

Unable to offer any relevant advice on entering the film industry, my Dad suggested I wrote a WHO WHAT WHY WHERE WHEN of my thoughts and ambitions as that was what he would do when asked to develop and deliver new ideas at ICI. I grimaced as I hated writing but, with cups of tea and cake provided by Mum, I put pen to paper and started to unfurl the questions.

I soon realised that each W word had a double meaning – *WHO am I?* doubled as *WHO did I want to be?* *WHAT have I done?* also became *WHAT was I trying to do?* and so on. I stuck with it and, after several days and lots of cups of tea later, I had written reams of hand-written scrawl. I proudly presented them to my Dad thinking he might give me the answer but he didn't even read them. He just told me to now whittle it down into a mission statement. Sigh.

I finally surfaced with eleven words.

"I want to change the face of the British film industry," I announced.

The statement startled me. It startled my Dad. Mum put the kettle on. Where had that come from? I thought I'd just wanted to be that woman in the studio making it happen, I hadn't expected to launch a revolution.

At the time I didn't even know what it meant but, if that was what many days of writing and whittling had produced, who was I to argue? I instinctively felt that whatever happened it would all work out for the best and, up to that point, I had enjoyed the twists and turns that my wonky path had taken me down so I wasn't too spooked by yet another dramatic turn. I trusted myself.

Thinking about it now, apart from the lack of confidence in my early years, I'd found my journey from leaving college, to the workplace and then setting up a company, pretty easy. Instinctive, in fact. Obvious, even. I knew I didn't possess the expected qualifications for success but I had definitely been blessed with some qualities that I believe can trump qualifications any day. Tenacity, instinct, drive, focus, passion, and the right work ethics were all vital to making the right decisions and delivering above expectation. And then, of course, I had a joker up my sleeve.

Dyslexia comes in many forms and effects everyone differently. For me it evolved from bad spelling, not being able to read aloud and retain information, to finally morphing into a completely unexpected form. Mine now came with a fast Intel in-brain processing chip. When confronted with a problem or challenge I was able to see an immediate solution. I see the wood and no trees. I go from A to Z without having to question nor worry about the B to Y. I am totally detail focussed which means I see every leaf on every tree in the wood.

So translating this into a work environment, I see all and miss nothing. It allows me to deliver everything I set out to do at a rather intense speed. It's like a superpower, albeit exhausting.

But every superpower comes with a dark side. At first, I thought everybody had a clear vision and could work at high speed without making mistakes. Back at work, I would become frustrated with colleagues who were unable to deliver within, what I thought, was a normal timeframe or not be able to match my attention to detail, which again I thought was on a normal scale. And I know that several entrepreneurs possess this intensity. Or are even possessed by it. This definitely makes it hard to 'fit in' as no one truly understands you.

I recognise now how my behaviour affected my work life and relationships. I'm sorry for unnerving my work colleagues as I sped through life leaving them behind, bobbing about in my wake, but at the time it constantly confused me. I couldn't understand why they couldn't keep up or why they seemed so startled by my deadlines. I didn't have anyone to talk to about it and no one to temper me. At home, after work, I'd wander around thinking *"But I'm meant to be the thick, lazy, stupid one. They've all been to Uni!"*

I sound like a nightmare, and I probably was, and I'm not proud of how I behaved but my actions and intentions were never malicious nor egotistical. I just had to get the job done. I had to deliver something creative, on time, on budget but, most importantly, above expectation. As I tended to be at the top of the pyramid leading a project, film or company all responsibility would fall on my shoulders and the pressure to handle all that would become too much. As my Dad would remind me *"It's lonely at the top, Janey,"* and he was right. I guess when you run your own company and live on your own you end up becoming a bit of a monster and no one there to tame the beast. After a while the pressure gauge blows.

Looking back at that young girl, standing in the kitchen, drinking tea with her parents, with an exciting new mission statement in hand, I wish I could have told her to recognise the rarity of such a superpower and how to manage it. I would have encouraged her to accept the speed in which other people work and to allow them to make their own mistakes. That would have saved a lot of pain from all sides.

But as a strong, confident woman, and I know that other strong, confident women will testify, it is too easy to be misinterpreted. Like that 'joke':

Q: *What's the difference between being assertive and being aggressive?*

A: *Your gender.*

Although I'm not sure I totally agree with the gender bit, as I've never felt 'female' in the workplace, but I do know that my behaviour has been constantly misunderstood and, over the years, it became increasingly harder for anyone to see my softer, kinder, caring interior behind this perceived hardened spiky shell. So, after a while, when people stop looking inside, I fought the fight alone, built the barriers wider and higher and the spikes became sharper.

My parents were the only people who could ever temper me, and I would always listen to them and try my best to learn and change. Over time I've definitely learned to slow down (a bit) but, by writing this, I've finally worked out that it was my extreme personality that pushed me over the edge and broke me. It's just a shame that no one around me seemed to care enough, nor took the time, to pull me back until it was too late.

But, in the same breath, I wouldn't want to adapt so much that I became average. Where's the adventure in that?!

FIVE

8th July: Pies, puddings and a wheel arch

PHOTO REFS C2 – C1

If I wasn't that tenacious, creative, driven, detail-focussed person I wouldn't be sitting in Charlie with Kenny, being waved off by a neighbour whose name I still don't know, about to go on a road trip of a life time! There are some things that I just wouldn't change.

•

Let the road trip begin...

Working out a route through England to Scotland was pretty overwhelming as there were so many options. In fact, when it comes to choosing and following road directions, I'd normally defer to someone else as I am a happier follower than a confident leader. Coupled with the fact that I had no clear idea of my destination, apart from going to Scotland via the Peak District, I started questioning every decision. But, as Lewis Carroll once said: *"If you don't know where you are going, any road will get you there."* So, with that in mind, I decided to get myself to the Peaks and make it up from there.

Google maps had estimated a four-hour drive to the Peak District so optimistically, leaving at 11am, I thought I'd get to my first campsite by 3pm. I drove the fastest route out of London and headed up the ugly M1. I do love a pork pie so I turned off the motorway at Oakham, with a plan for my first en route luncheon at the famous Melton Mowbray village. But time was already ticking away so it became a very quick pit stop in the village and I soon departed with a large pie and local cheese in hand bought from the perfectly named Ye Olde Pork Pie Shoppe. This was to become to my first evening meal on the road.

By the time I arrived at the campsite, I realised that I'd need to dramatically increase any Google map estimated journey time as Charlie tootles along at his own speed... no negotiation. I had been driving for over six hours. But all was good as I was greeted by one of my best friends who had come prepared to support my first night away with champagne and strawberries, which was my last taste of decadence during the trip. We built a fire and ate pie whilst I kept a watchful eye on Kenny as he ventured out of the van to feel the sensation of grass between his paws. It was a lovely first night.

In the morning, after breakfast, I waved my friend off and felt my first wave of nerves from the silence. It was all up to me now. I'd have to make all the decisions on my own. Deep breath. I've got this...

It would have been Dad's birthday today so I paused for thought. Dad was a big cyclist so, in honour of him, my first decision was to Lycra up, jump on the saddle and go for my first bike ride. I'd never gone on a solo ride before as I'd only ever gone on group rides so I was a little apprehensive venturing out on my own, mainly due to my lack of sense of direction. I know. Who in their right mind would go on a road trip with no sense of direction? ME!

From pies to puddings, I felt a theme of baked goods emerging so I headed for the oldest pie shop in Bakewell and was greeted with something that Mr Kipling had not prepared me for. A proper Bakewell pudding is a rather ugly, misshapen affair served hot with custard and jam on the side. Exceedingly naughty but bloody delicious. It was a short but steep ride home but, with sugar levels at a high, I powered up every hill back to the van.

When I got back I let a harnessed Kenny out for an afternoon prowl and, as a light rain began to fall, he soon found a comforting dry place under the van. Clever boy. Unbeknown to me, my first challenge was about begin.

I'm not a big reader. It normally takes me about four years to read a book as I get so easily distracted by the slightest thing, which is a definite down side to my dyslexia, but I'd hoped to get the chance to get some quality book time on the trip. A friend had recommended a trilogy by Peter May who wrote very atmospheric thrillers set in the Outer Hebrides so I thought I could prepare myself through literature. Typically, I didn't read the back cover properly and picked the wrong book as this one was set in Paris! *Merde.*

My reading had been peppered with checks on Kenny's whereabouts, which always revealed him still sitting happily under the van, the adventurer in him was yet to come out. The book was good and was an easy read so, with a few chapters now under my belt, I leaned under the van to say "*hi*" to Kenny but all I could see was his lead leading up into the under carriage of Charlie. Eh?! I climbed out of the van and gave the lead a little tug but it felt stuck on something. I crawled around to take a better look but the lead was definitely going upwards and it didn't feel like a soft furry animal at the other end of it. I walked around the other side of the van to get a bit closer and got on all fours and, with a final tug, an empty harness fell to the ground.

WTF?!! Where's Kenny? Day two and I'd lost my travel companion! I knew I couldn't, and wouldn't, be able to carry on without him. Panic. Don't Panic. Panic! I looked at the time and I had been reading for about an hour. Why now, of all times, was I able to concentrate on reading for so long! The farm was surrounded by fields, outhouses, trees, all sorts of hiding places and he could be anywhere. I clicked into practical mode and called my friend with the well-behaved camping cats as I knew she would calm me down. "*Don't panic!*" was her advice. "*He'll come back.*" Panic!

The rain started falling heavier as I searched the campsite and farm land. I looked around the van, in the van, on the van. I got on my back and crawled as far as I could under the van to where the harness had dropped. Charlie is very low slung so it felt like I was potholing, which was a sport I had decided never to participate in due to my dislike of confined spaces and fear of being trapped.

But then, as my eyes adjusted to Charlie's dark underbelly, I breathed a huge sigh of relief. From a dark corner above me, Kenny's tail slowly unfurled and touched the ground. My clever boy hadn't run away at all, he'd just found a safe, dry comfortable spot under the wheel arch. Cats love dark corners. The further I crawled I could see that he was exceedingly comfortable and had no intentions of moving. But it was getting dark so I had to work out a way of enticing him out from his safe place before night fell.

Googling only presented videos of heroic firefighters removing kittens from engines and I certainly wasn't quite ready to be a damsel in distress on day two. My caravanning neighbours had seen my legs sticking out from under the van and came over to offer help. Luckily, they were cat lovers and they popped back to their van and returned with tinned salmon and moral support.

After two hours of calling, poking and enticing, Kenny still wasn't moving. As a last resort, I was about to call up some firefighting heroes when all of a sudden, the waft of warm salmon à la tin must have hit a hungry nerve as Kenny coolly and calmly sauntered down from his newfound spot and demolished the fish. As soon as he'd finished, I was able to grab him and get him back in the van. My silver tabby, whose silver had now been replaced by dirt, was finally home. I gave him a bloody good brush until his silver stripes returned, tucked him up in bed and drank a bottle of port with my neighbours.

If that's day two how on earth are the other forty going to work out...

SIX

10th July: The plague and being air-cooled

Morning came and I awoke to find Kenny spooning my leg. It was such a reassuring sight as he then stretched out on his back with a big yawn with his mischievous whiskers all of a-twitch. He peered underneath the curtains perusing his land and I wondered what he was plotting. After a short constitutional around the van he came over for his usual ten-minute morning head rub and looked comfortable in his new surroundings. Panic well and truly over.

So, my first decision de jour was to leave the Peaks and head to the top of the North Pennines. It was going to be a long drive but I knew that if I could get that far in a day then I'd be crossing the Scottish border by then next morn.

I still chose a couple of scenic detours and stopped off in Eyam, a picture postcard village of stone houses with flowers overflowing from every walled garden. For such a beautiful place, it's hard to believe that it was home to such tragedy and courage during the Great Plague in 1665, but this was why I made a beeline to it. The story of Eyam is truly remarkable. Realising that the plague had started to spread through their village, and could possibly spread through Derbyshire, the whole village stoically quarantined themselves until every plague sufferer had died. Funnily enough, the idea of quarantine is not so peculiar to us anymore.

But my interest in Eyam dated back to my film days. I had worked with a writer and director on a feature film treatment called *The Wedding Dress* about this very subject. A tailor from Eyam had been commissioned to make a wedding dress for a wealthy client in London. Upon completion, the dress was delivered to the bride but, unbeknown to her, with an infected flea nestled in the elaborate stitching. With that tiny flea, the blackest of death began to spread. The film was underpinned by a tragic love story between our hero from Eyam and his lover who lived in the neighbouring village. But, sadly, like an unlucky plague victim, our wonderful film idea died a death. Though I still think there's life in that old filmic flea yet...

After Eyam, I headed up the A1 and finally swung a left at Richmond. I decided on this route as my Granny lived in Richmond, London, and the thought of our huge family parties in her house filled me with utter joy so I decided it would be an appropriate stop-off for a nice cuppa and a custard cream – Granny's favourite!

My immediate family is small but I have a big extended family. My Mum was one of ten children (Irish-English!) with six sisters and three brothers. Most of her siblings had one to three children each so I have 13 cousins in all. First cousins are great and, to me, they feel more like my brothers and sisters as we can all enjoy each other's company without any fighting or bickering. One cousin and I have wonderful weekly three-hour phone calls with an equal amount of tea or wine, depending on the time of call. My earliest memories of Granny's house in Richmond were of noise, laughter, adults, children, food, cigarettes and booze! Granny was wonderfully energetic and loved to show off and entertain her grandchildren by flicking the kitchen lights off with a high kick and washing her hair in fairy liquid which made it stand on end to our squeals of delight.

After tea in a café on the cobbled square, I chose another detour which certainly paid off. The B6277, south of Northumberland National Park, was the perfect route. Long winding roads, long straight roads, long undulating roads, long smooth roads right in the heart of our rural and agricultural country. As the only vehicle on the road, and with unspoilt views as far as my eye could see, I felt privileged to be there. It was as if this was my land. The sun shone, Charlie tootled, I sang and Kenny snored.

It was a hot day and even though a VW camper engine might be air-cooled they are known for getting pretty hot inside especially in the back. And the back was Kenny's domain. One piece of kit that I had bought prior to the trip was a little double fan with tilting heads powered off the cigarette lighter. So I rigged it up in the back to blow right at him. I now had an air-cooled engine with an air-cooled Kenny. Cool.

My favourite track of the day was *A Horse With No Name* by America. If you ever fancy clearing your mind and removing that incessant monkey chatter that goes on day in day out, then drive down the B6277 in a campervan singing a song about a nameless horse.

After another six-hour drive I'd made it north of the Northumberland National Park and settled down for the night in a rather nondescript campsite. It was only ever going to be a one-night affair so I didn't mind. I would be up and out early the next morn.

SEVEN

11ᵗʰ July: Cowboys and The Hard Loch Café

PHOTO REFS D5 – I5

I'd made it to Scotland! Hooray!

The famous town just north of the Scottish border is Gretna Green, made famous by young romantic elopers. I'd never been there so I thought I'd stop off to soak up the love in the air. Wow, what an odd place and possibly The Most Unromantic Place Ever. A grey village with a little church flanked by cheap B&Bs, all with signs offering en-suite bathrooms and proudly announcing in bigger letters that all rooms had TVs. Not quite the fairy-tale ending for two star-crossed lovers secretly crossing the border, vowing undying love and then encountering their first fight over the remote control.

I quickly jumped back into Charlie and began a rather long and functional drive towards Loch Lomond and the Trossachs National Park. I hoped that my two and a half hours of A roads through Glasgow would be rewarded by some true Scottish beauty.

Loch Lomond would be my first official loch so I was extra excited at the prospect. But the road that flanked the loch was uncomfortably busy and lined by tall trees that only teased views of the loch as I drove by. Trucks owned the road and had no tolerance for any other vehicles, especially 49-year-old ones. They'd loom up behind Charlie, bullying him to pull over, reminding me of the 1970s film *Duel*. Duly intimidated, we gave in every time and swayed in their wake.

Wild camping is legal in Scotland but around Loch Lomond you still need a permit. I pulled into a layby at the top of the loch to call up the permit holders but sadly they had already run out for the next couple of nights. Hmmm. This wasn't going very well. Undeterred, I remembered driving past a sign half way down the loch for a campsite at Luss so I headed back south for 10 miles. My heart sank a bit when I realised it was a Caravan Park, normally full of large motor homes and caravans. I started to worry that my dream road trip was not going to match my expectations. When I checked in I cheekily requested to park up in the most secluded corner of the campsite away from everyone else. They looked a bit surprised but luckily had one spot left.

It couldn't have been more perfect. My little parking spot was right on the shores of Loch Lomond and I had a little path leading to my own private loch-side beach. The afternoon sun shimmered on the water as I stepped out across the pebbled beach on to some large boulders protruding into the loch. I sat on the biggest boulder and just watched and listened to the water lapping up on the rocks for a while until hunger crept in. I suddenly thought *"Why don't I build my kitchen out here and cook outside?"*. So that's what I did. My twin-burning stove, gas, ingredients, wine, speaker and a cushion were all laid out on the rocks and I cooked and dined from there with ducks for company. Expectations well and truly exceeded.

•

I've never been one for beach holidays and have happily traded an all-over golden tan for a hardcore adventure. Living on a beach in Costa Rica building a turtle sanctuary for leatherbacks and olive ridleys; reaching 82° North on an Arctic voyage watching polar bears traverse the Arctic shelf or being transported through Switzerland and being taken up the Jungfrau on the Glacier Express, is my kinda thing. In fact, if I return without cuts, bruises, scars or frostbite from a holiday then I'm sorely disappointed.

In 2005, with only basic horse riding skills up my sleeve, I volunteered at a working cattle ranch in Montana for my summer holiday. It took around 50 cowboys, and of course cowgirls, to surround the 800 herd and move them gently to their summer pastures over eight days. We were in the saddle for eight hours a day come rain or shine, and indeed snow but the constant supply of bourbon definitely kept our spirits high.

In fact, I found out that if you drink a third of a litre of bourbon a day it's just enough to keep you warm and energised whilst hollering "*Move on!*" and "*Hey hey hey!*" at the cows and calves all day long. These instructions were interspersed with chasing the odd runaway calf as it bolted from the herd. I'm still not sure where they thought they were going but a cowgirl's job was to gallop after the escapee and bring him back into the fold. Yee haaaw indeed! I now know how to line dance and lasso the hind legs of a runaway calf – a skill I've not yet needed since my return.

At the end of a long day, the army-style campsite was always set up ahead of our arrival and we would all sit together around a huge fire listening to cowboy stories, singing songs, drinking the remains of the bourbon whilst eating steak and refried beans.

On one sunny day, whilst looking out over the herd under Montana's big sky, one of the cowboys cantered up beside me and said "*You know Ma'am, it don't get much better than this.*" Well Mr Cowboy, I beg to differ...

My Cheshire Cat smile stretched across my face as I sat on my rock on the loch with my makeshift kitchen griddling fresh Scottish salmon bought from the local smokehouse, dipping my feet into the cool Lomond waters, drinking wine, knowing I've got several weeks of this ahead of me.

As I ate, a new song came up on Spotify radio: *Slow It Down* by Crowes Pastures. I'd never heard it before but it said it all. It summed me up perfectly and I played it on repeat. I was slowing down and I could already feel it. My thoughts were slower, my world was slower, my breathing was slower and deeper.

For the first time I really felt the muddied waters in my mind clearing. Already, there were fewer thoughts in my head. Just seeing and being.

Eating and drinking. Looking and seeing. Making things up. No plans. No spreadsheets. No guilt. Just silence. I was the only customer in my very own Hard Loch Café and I sat there for hours certainly not feeling alone and, for the first time in a long time, not feeling lonely.

EIGHT

Why would a lonely person go on a solo road trip?

When I first announced to my friends that I was about to embark on a solo road trip, I expected to hear *"Oh how exciting!"* or *"Wow, where are you going?"* but no, the main response was *"Oh, you're so brave."*

Brave? Why would I be brave? This wasn't about bravery. I wasn't going to war. My life wasn't at risk. So why did people think that my solo travels were going to be an act of bravery? Was it because they thought that solo meant alone and that alone meant lonely and therefore someone would have to be brave to face loneliness head on?

But hang on, I *was* lonely, so the question of why would a lonely person go on a solo trip is worthy of interrogation.

For a long time, it's a question I've worked hard to answer for myself and worked even harder to overcome. Loneliness is misunderstood, not just because it is too readily confused with being alone, but because it is still such a social taboo. It is, without doubt, one of people's biggest fears which makes it hard to even have an open conversation about it with friends when loneliness strikes.

Trust me I've tried. Without realising, friends have shut the conversation down and I can see it in their eyes. That flash of *"Thank God it's not me,"* as I'm am offered suggestions like *"Why don't you join a group?"* or *"How about starting a hobby with other people?"* Sorry but these couldn't be more unhelpful to someone feeling lonely. Nevertheless I hold my nerve, smile and say that I'll look into it, which I don't. But to be honest, it's not up to my friends to find the solution for me.

As a single woman who lives on her own I know the difference between being alone and loneliness. The former is under my control and the latter is out of my control.

I'm lucky that I enjoy my own company and can even make myself laugh. Even though it is assumed I am an extrovert I am in fact an introvert, which in itself is another misunderstood trait. I choose to recharge my batteries alone and can potter for hours in my house without the need to call anyone, go out or have to meet people in order to feel happy or energised. I choose to be alone and therefore I am in control of it. If I didn't want to be alone I would join a group.

However, when loneliness rears its head, which, confusingly, can also be an irrational feeling that grows out of control, it manifests itself as a sense of utter sadness through isolation, a feeling of abandonment, being forgotten or having a complete lack of connection to other people, even your friends. Even though I have a large network of friends, I could go for days without anyone even calling me which made the isolation even greater and the silence unbearable. And it wouldn't be mitigated by *me* calling them as all I needed was to be remembered by *them*. Therefore a lonely person cries out in silence for attention. As *I* cannot change this situation or feeling, it is out of my control. However, a call from a friend or an invitation to dinner solves this immediately and wipes the white board, covered in negative thoughts, clean.

Our inescapable digital world only exacerbates the problem by encouraging lonely people to broadcast their own fake news of faux connection, friendship and happiness to all. It's not helping. I don't fall into this bracket but in extreme cases it's like digital self-harm. Instead of hiding cuts under a hemline, someone can live the lie of pretending to be happy by posting manipulated pictures of perceived beauty with groups of friends who they may not even connect with. Either way they still feel invisible and, instead of using the pain of cutting to feel alive, they hold out for any reassurance through a 👍 or a 🖤. During these moments it's almost impossible for anyone to reach out, be honest or ask for help so it can easily become the beginning of a spiral down.

I've tried to be open and honest about my loneliness, though whenever I have had the chance to start a conversation with friends about it I am also reminded that *"people in relationships can be lonely too, you know."* Yes, I know, but this is where control comes back in to the equation. Unless someone is in an abusive relationship where fear keeps them there, then they do have the freedom of choice to leave. Though I wonder if a lonely person in a relationship chooses to stay because the thought of being lonely *and* alone feels worse, so they choose, what they believe is, the lesser of two evils.

A couple of years ago I converted my one bedroom flat into a two-bedroom maisonette and commissioned a designer to create a staircase. Rather than a means to go up and down stairs he proposed to make something similar to an art installation. (Well, if you're going to put in a staircase you might as well put in a *staircase*). My wooden spiral called Nautilus is a remarkable piece of design and engineering and I'm delighted to spend more time admiring its form than watching the telly. However, it soon became a physical reminder of my loneliness.

I knew that if I fell down my perfectly formed stairs on a Friday night then I'd probably not be found till the following Tuesday at the earliest because there wasn't one person who regularly called me, or checked-in, or was a constant presence in my life. I just didn't have that support network in place. Work would probably just wonder where I was on the Monday and do nothing about it thinking that I was probably working from home. I know this to be true as once I had been ill on a Monday unable to call or reply to their work-related emails or texts but my work colleagues, who were only a three-minute walk away from my home, did nothing and just wondered from their desks where I was. I guess to them I was just their bossy boss so why would they care.

Without a partner to have daily contact there was no one to miss me. My friends were understandably busy with their own lives and, in fact, all assumed that I had it covered. People tend to paint their own picture or make assumptions on someone else's life and, because they seemed to think that I was always out and about with a busy social life, which I wasn't, they wouldn't want to interrupt me. I couldn't exactly ask my friends to check up on me every day. No one likes a needy person so I just had to do that British thing and keep calm and carry on and, without trying to pretend to be OK, I had to be OK.

But, the idea of lying at the bottom of my award-winning stairs for days, not being able to move with my phone just out of reach, or even lying there dead, with no one looking through the letterbox calling *"Janey? Are you OK?"* made me shudder. *Dreams Of A Life* is documentary that unravels the story of a young woman who lay dead in her home for three years, in London, without being found. Three years! In London! She was popular, charismatic and had several groups of friends but none of them missed her assuming she was out and about with social circle. Her body literally dissolved away through time and they could only identify her through her teeth and a photo of her smiling they found in her home. How horrific is that?

I guess that's another reason for lonely people to stay in a bad relationship, at least if they fall downstairs their partner will hear them, find them and save them.

We've been indoctrinated into believing that the *married with children* model offers ultimate happiness and fulfilment so everyone chases it. Whenever I reveal that I am a single woman in her fifties with no children I always get that patronising head tilt to the side, like a dog, with an *"Oh, I'm sorry,"* added on for good measure. Fuck off! What are you sorry about? It's actually great being single!

So, let's just flip that happiness and fulfilment coin for one second shall we to remind ourselves of the positives of being single with no kids. What you get is absolute independence, the freedom to make decisions without debate, the ability to solve your own problems, the confidence to find your own solutions and the chance to wallow in 'me' time!

It's funny, when I was right in the middle of the major works on my flat the pressure of solo decision making was taking its toll and I started thinking that it might have been easier with a partner. I remember saying to a friend ruefully *"It's so stressful having to make all the decisions on my own,"* and then I stopped and thought: *"Hang on, I actually get to make all the decisions on my own!"* And with that slight difference of inflection and perspective, my image of freedom and independence burst from monotone to technicolour.

So, no, I wasn't brave to go on a solo trip, I was in fact indulging in the opportunity to make my own decisions, to breathe deeply and entertain silence, to build my own fires and to get lost without anyone telling me I was lost. Ultimate freedom!

NINE

13th July: Rest And Be Thankful

PHOTO REFS D4 – F4

And it was that very freedom that I was lapping up at Loch Lomond.

After two silent nights, I left my private Idaho at first light and followed the A83 north. I drove along the pass that divides Glen Kinglas from Glen Croe alongside the old winding military road which climbed to 800 feet. Not a dramatic altitude I know but when I reached the top it was enough to be rewarded with an unbroken view of the historic valley below. This route is named Rest And Be Thankful and what a perfectly wonderous name for a valley. Some say it was named by the soldiers who built the road in 1750 when they were allowed to finally rest after its completion.

I parked up at the top and opened my sliding door to look down on the valley and two roads below. I was starving but didn't feel like firing up my kitchen. Wouldn't it be amazing if there was a café at the top of this wilderness... I reminded myself to keep managing my expectations... oh hang on... there was one! And it was open for business! It was a family run mobile café and their hot plates were sizzling with bacon, eggs and Scottish Lorne square sausages. The air was filled with a scent good enough to turn a vegan. I ordered my first square sausage and egg bap and washed it down with a steaming hot cuppa. Kenny and I sat in the van and gazed down on the valley for some time. I reflected on being a most grateful 52 year old and by the concentration on Kenny's face I could see he was scanning through his eighteen months on this earth with gratitude.

In the end, I thanked myself for giving myself permission to take this time off and just stop and enjoy the silence. What a fucking luxury.

My life had definitely become full of noise. Everyone's life is. Working, talking, listening, eating, drinking, watching, cycling, doing. All of which are great things to do in moderation but as a constant it just became too much. No pause. No off button. No time out.

And now, with my pause button well and truly pressed down, I had time to think, work things out, file thoughts away and to allow new thoughts in.

I pressed play on Ludovico Einaudi's *Fuori Dal Mondo* and reflected on the middle part of my career and how it had formed the woman I had become today. The film industry certainly allowed me to indulge in some mega highs but hadn't spared me the pain of dealing with the equally mega lows.

TEN

Short films and red carpets

After my own calling to Change The Face Of The British Film Industry, I thought I'd better work out how to go about it, even though I still wasn't entirely sure what it meant.

The chasm between producing 30-second commercials and 90-minute features was vast so I decided to start with a more achievable leap by producing 10-minute short films and learn the ropes from there.

Phase one started with securing scripts, so I reached out to a then very small pool of filmmakers in Manchester and read as many scripts as I could. It didn't take long to realise that a great script pretty much punches you in the face when you read it and, for me, the ones that packed the biggest punches all had strong social themes. I didn't realise at the time but my social conscience, like a sleeping dragon, was beginning to stir.

It took me a few months to secure my first two scripts. One was a black comedy and the other, a hard hitting piece of social drama with an ending that literally made me fall off my chair when I read the final scene. Both scripts were attached to commercials directors that I had previously worked with and the latter was from the original director who had encouraged me all that time ago. Of course, they were both delighted when I offered to raise the finance and get their films made.

So, on to phase two, raising the finance. I was happy to live off my modest savings for as long as possible to keep me going but I needed production funds. I had initially read, albeit my dyslexic version, about how to raise film finance via tax incentives. Something to do with investors, something to do with an Enterprise Investment Scheme and something to do with £150,000, so my immediate thought was to raise this cash and allow £50k per film and make three films. Ridiculously, that was the extent of my understanding, but based on that idea, I decided to sell equity in Silver Films to investors to raise the production funds needed to make the films.

I then bravely (though in retrospect, I'm not quite sure that is the right word) decided to give my directors, and the films, my undivided attention so I chose to stop all commercial activity to focus on film production. My reasoning being was that the sooner I could finish the shorts, the quicker I could start producing feature films. But this meant saying goodbye to all my clients and revenue which then reduced the valuation of my company to zero. My fantastical plans were developing so quickly I hadn't quite considered that a company's valuation is key to raising investment.

The other tricky factor was that short films don't make a profit so I knew that this initial investment would never render a return. This would have to be pitched as the Research and Development phase rather than the need for production funding. I'd need to emphasise that this would create intellectual property and traction in order for the company to move towards making feature films. Only then, would a return on investment would be possible. It definitely was a long-term plan.

I mooted my finger-in-the-air idea to a couple of producer friends who rather condescendingly told me that it would never work.

"*Investors don't invest in short films,*" they snorted.

"*But my model is to get investors to invest in the production company not the short films...*" I explained to deaf ears.

Undeterred, I approached the local North West Business Angel Network to see if I could present at one of their quarterly investor meetings. Even though I was paying for the privilege, I still had to convince them that I was a serious contender. They listened and sighed, then smiled and said: "*Our investors don't do film... but you seem like a nice fun girl so we could put you on before the break as some light relief. Oh, and maybe wear a skirt and stand in front the podium so that they can see your legs.*" I paid my money, prepared my PowerPoint and positioned myself firmly behind the podium in trousers. You may be wondering why I didn't protest about this blatant sexism but this was the '90s, where comments like this were par for the course, so I carried on regardless.

This was the first time I had ever spoken in public since my debut as the Reindeer in *The Snow Queen* at the age of seven; dressed in thick dark brown tights, a matching brown polo neck jumper and papier mâché antlers that leaned to one side I delivered a quivering *"No one ever goes further north than this"* so quietly that no one could hear. After weeks of rehearsing with my family my acting career ended there. My sister was the performer in the family, the confident one, so presenting to a room of investors was the kind of thing that she could do without preparation but for me this was going to be the most terrifying performance imaginable. At least I wasn't wearing thick brown tights and wonky antlers!

Before I went on, I locked myself in the toilet for half an hour pacing and muttering to myself wondering how I'd got myself into this in the first place and why I even thought I could get away with it.

The time came and I presented my idea in a dry corporate room full of even drier investors – a bit like *Dragon's Den*, but before 'Dragons' existed. There were about 50 of them lined up in theatre style seats. It didn't start well. As soon as I mentioned the word 'film' they all pretty much looked down, shuffled their papers and ignored me. To be fair, I had been warned.

My Dad was proudly sitting in the back of the room and, sensing I was losing the room he mouthed something at me. I stopped my presentation and said: *"I just thought I'd let you know that my Dad is at the back of the room telling me to smile, so..."*

I paused. They looked up. I smiled. And with that, I got the room back. My final slide recapped my speech by saying that this investment was going to be long-term, high-risk but potentially lots of fun.

"Any questions?" I nervously asked hoping they wouldn't ask me about the value of my company. After tumbleweed had drifted through the

room and the clocks had chimed, a hand went up. It was from a veteran investor with wild white hair sporting a colourful bow tie and a wry smile.

"*And what is the current value of your company?*" he asked knowing the answer.

With a brave but forced smile I replied. "*Zero.*"

"*Correct!*" he said and then, to my utter surprise, he went on to arrange our first meeting.

Really? An angel investor wanted to take this to the next stage and discuss the possibility of him funding my short films? Extraordinary! Hilarious even! Had a nervous girl with a dream just captured an investor's eye? It couldn't be that easy, could it? I didn't tell anyone that about our forthcoming meeting just in case it wasn't going to be that easy.

We met a week later and he was absolutely delightful. He explained that investors invest in people not just the project and went on to admit that he had been intrigued by my honesty, passion and smile and therefore wanted to come on board to "*have a bit of fun.*" And with that, together with the sound of people saying to me "*that'll never work*" still ringing in my ears, we signed the deal and he became my first business angel. He was highly respected in the investment world so, based on his calibre and belief in me, two other angels joined in my long-term, high-risk world of entertainment.

An equity deal that raised funding to produce short films had never been secured before which pricked the ears of my peers in the industry and the doubters started to take note. I carried on to successfully negotiate matched funding deals with Fox Searchlab and regional film agencies funded by The National Lottery and then finally secured sponsorship and product placement deals from my friends in the games industry. In the end, I did indeed raise around £150k.

From the date of the initial presentation to banking all the investment took around six months but I'd done it! I'd banked enough finance to make some short films. I'd just changed the way short films could be funded. With my mission statement embedded in my brain, I beamed, took a deep breath, kept calm and, as my Dad would always say, "*Just get on with it!*" So I did and merely wondered where my wonky path would take me next.

•

The short film world was a truly wonderful world to inhabit and if I could have made a living from it, as in earned any money from it, I would have done so in a heartbeat. But sadly, their place in this world is not to earn revenue. Their purpose is to raise awareness of the film makers to the industry via international film festivals, competitions, and intense networking. If these parts are in place, and a film is good enough to be accepted onto the festival circuit or indeed win an award, then that can aid a smoother transition into the feature film world.

Short filmmaking is also rather indulgent as it gives you that rare freedom to tell the story that you want to tell and the chance to move and engage an audience free from an advertising client requesting "*Can we have our logo bigger?*" or any film financiers who have the power to cut scenes if they feel the film is going over budget.

The first film I shot was a black comedy called *Jump*. The location was on three opposing rooftops right in the heart of Soho. Our casting director had done a sterling job by securing some really great names including John Thompson, Andy Serkis, Sanjeev Bhaskar and Freddie 'Parrot-Face' Davies. 'Where you fall is where you stay' was the strapline for the film as all our characters were ghosts who had jumped, or been pushed, off their ledge. Apart from our lead (John) who was attempting to jump from Freddie's roof, but that was against The Rules. One jumper per roof. The ghosts from neighbouring rooftops managed to talk John down, only for him to (spoiler alert) get knocked over by a bus. A fun, frivolous film that health and safety wouldn't allow by today's standards as John was harnessed to the edge of the roof three storeys high!

The second film was *About A Girl* and took a more social tone. A perfectly written monologue of a 13-year-old girl walking down a canal in Manchester chatting about her life, hopes and dreams. Based on a true story that the writer had seen in The Guardian, its horrific outcome was enough to silence a cinema audience with only intakes of breath to be heard. This was only the second piece of film that our lead actress had done and her delivery of the verbatim script was utterly compelling. This was also the script that received the most rejections from funders, one saying: *"It's not really a film is it? It doesn't have a traditional act one, act two, act three. The best short films are comedies. I suggest you concentrate on that genre."* I didn't take Film4's advice on that occasion.

Some people set out to make films to win awards. I set out to make the best films I could. My aim was to produce films that I believed in and cared about. I concentrated on ground-breaking social issue films that would emotionally engage an audience enough to make them think beyond leaving the cinema and going for a pizza. Films that could raise debate, open discussions and change opinion were the films that I was going to make. *Jump* was a fun first film, but all my other films had a social drama at their core.

But then *About A Girl* did start to win... we won the Edinburgh Film Festival, we were the only British short screened at Sundance, where I met the lovely, though smaller than expected, Robert Redford. We won the BAFTA for Best Short Film, where I met the Hollywood glitterati and got to thank *"...my Mum, my Dad and my family and friends!"* on stage and live on TV. *Teenage Kicks* by The Undertones was our walk-up track and hearing it again will always take me back to that long walk down the aisle to the stage trying not to trip in a long dress and heels. The film continued winning numerous international awards and ended up being heralded as one of the most successful short films of its time. I still meet film students from around the world who studied it as an example of brave film making.

Because of my unique funding route and my bravery of backing such an unusual script, I was invited to talks and flown out to industry panels at international film festivals where wannabe film-makers would interrogate me in the hopes of emulating my early path. But they'd ask the wrong questions.

"*How do you feel about being a female producer in the industry?*" one young woman asked me.

"*I'm not a female producer,*" I replied to a slightly startled female audience. "*I'm a producer. Don't label yourself, just do your job.*" I then told them not to follow anyone else's path, they needed to carve their own groove and develop their own instinct as to what was right and what was wrong.

Finally, my parents understood what I did for a living and could not have been prouder. I too was proud that my home-grown instinct had taken me down this red-carpeted path. It was a feeling that none of us had experienced in relation to my earlier non-achievements so we all indulged in it. To feel proud, without ego, is a remarkably powerful feeling. It burst out of me in the form of confidence and energy. I could see the muddied waters of the feature film world clearing as I knew that I could now fully trust my intuition and that my instincts would take me down a straighter, and hopefully, more direct path.

But it's desperately sobering how quickly a bubble can burst. And, to be honest, my bubble began bursting the morning after winning the BAFTA.

The press calls were coming in and TV interviews were being requested but, bizarrely, the director refused to do any. He wanted to do them in his own time and wouldn't listen when I said that old news is no news. And to be honest we weren't even that big a news. "*It's all about you, isn't it Janey?*" he said sarcastically, naively misunderstanding the role of a producer who not only makes the film but has to market the film and the team! So, on behalf of the film *and* the team, I then had to do solo live links to regional TV stations, radio and manage the press.

Bear in mind that this was the very same director who I had worked for and who had encouraged me ten years earlier, and who I had also called a friend for many years. He stopped taking any of my calls but chose to send me an email instead. It was the cruellest piece of writing I could have ever read. In fact it became the second time I fell of my chair whilst reading. It was a totally out-of-the-blue character assassination that must have been building up in him for months, whilst I was funding and making *his* film!

And there was I thinking we had the dream team of director / writer / producer ready to hit the feature film world together. But no. He shot me down and left me for dead. He dumped me, removed the Silver Films logo from the copies of the film he sent out and used that to further his own career. It was a cowardly thing for him to have done by not confronting me face to face and I still wish to this day that he could have talked to me. We have never spoken since.

It was an enormous blow for me and stopped me in my tracks. A BAFTA-winning director is immediately picked up and offered scripts, and he was. A BAFTA-winning producer, abandoned by a director, has to start again, so I did. Fuck him.

It took a while but I picked myself up and found another director for the third in my trilogy of short films. *Talking With Angels* was shot the following year and portrayed the disturbing but true story of the director's childhood. He was brought up in a 1970s racist Salford by his obese mother who suffered from schizophrenia and who turned to prostitution to support her ever-growing number of mixed-raced children. The film was seen through the eyes of the eldest ten-year-old son and we cast and shot it on the near derelict Langworthy Estate in Salford, the very one where he had lived.

It was a brutal film and equally brutal to make. Reliving his horrifying past on celluloid, surrounded by a crew, completely broke the director and all of us around him. He almost turned feral. However, this extraordinary power and emotion was captured on film and this short was nominated for a BAFTA and proved to be another hit on the short film circuit.

•

I'd now produced two award-winning short films, albeit traumatic in theme and experience, and was now in a position where I was unable to continue with either directors. I needed to readdress my approach. I was confident in my ability to pick the right scripts so I cut to the chase and set about looking for a feature script, without realising that it's a rarity to be offered a ready-to-go script. One needs to live in Development Hell for several years before emerging with a self-funded final draft of a 90+ page script that a financier may choose to look at, if the wind is in the right direction.

The first project I picked up on was in the form of a treatment, which is just a 25-page pre-script outline of the film. It was a lovely feel-good story of a young boy from Liverpool who dreamed of becoming a bull fighter. But then *Billy Elliot* came out. Liverpool had been replaced by Newcastle and the bulls by ballet shoes. Apart from that it was pretty much identical but I had to let that go.

Literary agents had started sending me books but as this was the longest development path to tread it wasn't my priority. And it also meant that I had to read the whole book!! Reading treatments and scripts were fine for me but a whole book…? Please!

But then the oddest of books crossed my path. *Nalda Said,* written by Stuart David of Belle & Sebastian fame. It was out of print but had been translated into many languages so I surmised it had wide appeal. I read it in one go. This was it. I was utterly and completely in love with it! With no sense of location nor timeframe it was a gorgeously bizarre tale of a young boy brought up by his gypsy Aunt Nalda. He believed the fantastical, metaphorical stories she told him as a child that she had used to explain the world to him. He grew to be a confused and terrified young man, constantly on the run, assuming every stranger would cut him open to find the jewel within him.

I took out an exclusive option on the book, which meant that no other producer could develop it and, for the next seven years, I worked tirelessly with writers to turn the book into a screenplay. Nothing had prepared me for how hard this was going to be nor how long this would take. And nothing had prepared me for how it would drain my finances.

Enter Development Hell... Seven years of drafts, re-writes, discussions, debates, tears, starting over, new writers, re-writes, new drafts... It was amazing how long I stayed focussed whilst just about managing to survive by living off my ever-depleting savings. But when my focus started to falter, and I started getting hungry, I started to worry. It's a mega tough decision to let something you love go. Especially when it's been a dream for so long, when you've got so close you can touch it and especially when you still have a crazy mission statement rattling around in your head.

The thing that kept me going were the tales I'd heard about other filmmakers living on beans for years in order to fight for their vision and then, as they're scraping the last bean from the last tin they got the deal of all deals to become the overnight success that took them ten years in the making. It's as addictive as gambling. Just one more draft, one more meeting, just one more week, just one more tin of beans...

But *one more* wasn't keeping the wolf from the door anymore and I'd completely run out of beans. I made the toughest business decision to furlough the script and resurrect the commercial arm of Silver Films to create an income stream. I knew this would be a distraction from the script but, in the end, it turned out to be a bloody good decision.

I brought in a wonderful commercials director as my business partner and, somehow, together, we found a niche shooting cars around the world. Still to this day I don't know how we pulled that off but the stars aligned and we started making money. We were also able to pay back some of the investment to the Angels so it was a win-win situation.

Filmmaking was high on his agenda too and he was also in love with *Nalda Said* so we both shared a vision and created a new mantra: *To shoot cars to feed the bank and make films to feed the soul.*

With a new writer attached we had the perfect trio to resurrect Nalda. We had already established that we all worked really well together in the commercial world but, as all emerging film directors need a short film under their belt as their calling card, we made the decision together to fund a short film with profits from our company.

Gardens With Roses was another social drama with a young couple at its heart. Like a modern day Bonnie and Clyde they would infiltrate a vulnerable elderly person's home and steal their money, possessions and medication before moving on to their next elderly victim. Sadly, this is another true story which happens all too often. Once the film was made we gifted it to the charity Action for Elder Abuse and they used this powerful drama to raise awareness, change policy and raise funding.

Finally, a director/producer relationship that was successful! Together with the writer, we began serious development of *Nalda Said*. It felt great to be back in the driving seat again with a team that harmonised. We were off!

The film industry is called an industry for a reason. Its motivation is to make money and all eyes are on the first weekend box office figures. I was at a film-making seminar once where we were asked:

"What is the most important document in getting a film made?"

I shot my hand up immediately. *"The script!"* I said confidently.

"No," was the immediate reply and a haunting sensation of a hard slap on my thigh was felt as I wondered if I'd inadvertently shouted out *"Cow!"*

"It's the document outlining the recoupment window for the investors."

Well, that rather took the shine off things. So much for creativity. So much for engaging with an audience. So much for the power of film being able to make a difference. So much for investing everything you have and going hungry to make a film you believe in. As a collective sigh exhaled around the room I could see my dreams float out of the window. If only I'd realised earlier that arthouse films are almost impossible to fund as they do not recoup enough at box office. It's easier to raise £100m for a stupid rom-com than it is to raise £1m for a social drama.

After a couple more years of touting our script, my director and I had to face the stark truth that we'd backed the wrong horse. I didn't want to go through Development Hell on yet another project and, for me, the reality of just shooting cars and producing commercials wasn't enough. It felt like a natural chapter was coming to an end and I agreed with my instincts. We signed my director up with another production company so he was sorted. And me? I closed the book on my film career.

As I sat alone in our emptied production office and thought about that woman from the photograph in her empty studio. I felt a sense of calm wash over me. I reflected on what I had achieved. It was off the scale compared to my expectations. What's reassuring for anyone else holding on to an impossible dream, is that as soon as I let it go – with no regrets and no 'if onlys' – I was miraculously able to move on immediately, free from any sense of failure, but with a feeling of pride knowing that I couldn't have tried any harder. However, the key to moving on completely is to completely let go in order for another wonky path to be revealed.

For all their divine wisdom the nuns could never have predicted that their "*thick and lazy schoolgirl*" would actually amount to something. That she would set up a company, travel the world, become an expert in the gaming and automotive industries, produce films that still make a difference to society and walk down two red carpets rubbing shoulders with the Hollywood glitterati.

I never did change the face of the British film industry. But I had a bloody good go at it and, however hard it was, it couldn't have been more fun. If that's not amounting to something, or in fact making it, then I don't know what is. Take that nuns!

ELEVEN

14th July: Leaping salmon and rush hour traffic

PHOTO REFS G4 – F3

If it hadn't been for the darkest of tunnels and the brightest of spotlights I wouldn't be here now, and for that I was thankful. I closed my eyes. One final deep breath in and one final calm breath out. Let it all go. Eyes open. Click. I took a mental photo of the Rest and Be Thankful valley and took note of how I felt. I could have stayed there for hours but felt thoroughly sated with my hour's rest. I knew I needed to get some miles on the clock so I jumped back in the driver's seat whilst Kenny assumed his position squeezed under the passenger seat.

I retraced my tracks back towards the top of Loch Lomond and headed north, via the monstrous Ben Nevis to my right and towards the mythical monster within Loch Ness. My track of the day as I approached the Loch was *Swamp Thing* by The Chameleons in honour of the thing that never was. The only beasts that did make an appearance that afternoon were the coachloads of tourists sporting Nessie merch and tartan selfie sticks.

The road that flanks Loch Ness heads north to the medieval town of Inverness. When you look on a map it's like someone tried to cut the top of Scotland off at a 45° angle with a blunt knife, with Inverness hanging on by a thread. It's not a big city, but to me it suddenly felt huge and bustling. I had traffic lights and junctions to negotiate, people and cars to avoid... all too much for this little solo traveller, so I got out as soon as I could.

Inverness is also the start and end point for the North Coast 500. Even though I knew I wouldn't be following the whole route, I realised

I'd have to stick to it for a little while as I travelled clockwise, so, over Kessock Bridge I went and headed west to the coast.

By now it was getting late and I hadn't even eaten anything since my square sausage nor looked for anywhere to stay. After driving away from civilisation I realised I was also running very low on petrol. Bearing in mind that the needle on Charlie's petrol gauge dances around merrily depending on whether he is driving uphill, downhill or over a bump, you never quite know how much fuel you have left, but I knew that I'd have to address this pretty soon. I normally got in a habit of filling him up when the needle hovered around half full but petrol stations are not as plentiful in rural Scotland. I thought I'd be clever and do a Google search for *'petrol stations near me'* and, after a nine-mile detour, it guided me towards a derelict petrol pump in the middle of nowhere. Grrrrr. Tired, hungry and potentially out of fuel this did not make for a happy lass.

Out of the three, I knew which one required priority attention. My stomach. I definitely needed fuelling before Charlie, and cooking was not going to be an option, so I drove until I found the first place to eat. I was already looking like a traveller as they seated me in the corner, away from the other diners. It felt a bit odd eating fish and chips in a posh restaurant, on what also looked like date-night based on the number of couples around me holding hands and gazing at each other over their mushy peas. As I devoured one of my favourite meals the hangry feeling dissipated and I could focus again.

The lady in the restaurant kindly gave me my two remaining pieces of information in the right order. A petrol station on the way to a campsite. Fuelled up. Parked up in the dark. Tucked up in bed, I wondered if I was lucky enough to have a view of a river in the Riverview Campsite.

•

My alarm clock called Kenny woke me early and the opened curtains revealed the River Blackwater five feet from my windscreen. How lovely.

Even though I had come well prepared, to my joy, not a single midge had yet made an appearance. They normally go crazy near rivers but it looked like we were in for a midge-free morning. I could sense Kenny's disappointment as he had been most excited by the prospect of a mist of flying fun to dive in to. Like a locked-on missile he'd launch himself at anything with tiny wings and take them down. I guess flies are an indoor cat's mouse. From the warnings I had been seeing via my regular checks on the Smidge website – which kindly shows you areas to avoid based on the intensity of midges – I feared he may wear himself out early during our travels but this was not to be the case at Riverview.

My side door opened on to my neighbours and, with tea in hand, I said my hellos. To my right was a small group of enthusiastic fishermen cooking up a hearty breakfast. They told me about a must-see ferocious waterfall nearby called Rogie Falls where the salmon were leaping upstream to spawn. I agreed. To my left were a lovely couple who were cycling and camping across Scotland (now, that's brave!) who also wanted to see this rare sight, so the three of us jumped in Charlie and we drove off to find the forest, the waterfall and watch the preamble to the most unusual fate for these extraordinary fish. Born, migrate, mate, spawn, die. What a rotten hand to have been dealt by nature. They are delicious though!

The Rogie Falls were a fierce force of nature indeed and from a narrow, rickety wooden bridge stretching across the white waters we witnessed what I'd only ever seen on telly. Like muscles with fins, against all odds and science, these fish would literally fly upwards through torrents of white water. It was magical. Kenny would have been intrigued but sadly he had to stay guarding the van!

I dropped my cycling buddies back at the campsite and we said our goodbyes and followed each other on Insta. I headed west where the single-track roads and blind summits drew me to Applecross, a place that had been repeatedly recommended and, in fact, friends of mine had got engaged there. I approached the famous, albeit notorious, Bealach na Bà pass, the shortcut to Applecross, but it had just been closed. The extreme beauty of the pass is equal to its danger. Novice drivers are warned away whilst the determined experienced ones are put to the test. I would have loved to have driven it but the sound of the mountain rescue sirens negotiating the hairpin bends in the distance made it all too real. I heard later that there had been two separate motorbike accidents, both serious. These are dangerous roads.

Instead, I drove anti-clockwise over the top coastal road to get to my destination. I was looking forward to my first sight of white sands. I'd been told many times about the iconic white beaches on the west coast of Scotland and how the white sands have travelled up through the gulf stream from the Caribbean. *"Yeah yeah, I'm sure they're lovely,"* I'd always thought, *"but it's not going to look like the Caribbean."* WRONG! These beaches are better, cleaner, brighter than any Caribbean, tropical or exotic land. AND they're totally empty.

The drive over the top still needed 100% concentration as the roads were extremely narrow and steep. The frustration of being the sole driver is that it's hard to take in the beauty of your surroundings whilst negotiating the wheel. But when I did get a moment to soak it up, the vast expanse of dramatic undulating scenery made me feel like a little toy car driving in a giant's land. It's fun to physically feel one's perspective changing.

But then I hit rush hour. In Scotland, the Highland cows take priority on the roads and are allowed to loiter as and when they choose. Who was I to argue when a herd of beasts sat in the middle of the road? I pulled into a layby and watched them watch me through their overgrown fringes. In the layby I met a couple, of the human variety and about my age, in another van who parked up behind me. I think the husband was intrigued to see who was behind Charlie's wheel and did seem surprised when I popped out on my own. Female solo drivers, especially with a cat, are a very rare breed indeed, hence they attract a lot of attention.

Theirs was a modern van conversion - in fact the majority of campers are converted transits, all handcrafted and built to fulfil their personal travelling dreams. Showers, toilets, kitchens, creature comforts, raised double bed with the back double doors offering views of the wild. Lovely, but not my kinda thing. Charlie's vintage charm suited me down to the ground and he was most definitely a minority on the Scottish roads, which was another aspect I loved.

We chatted as we photographed the reclining cows. I got a measure of them pretty quickly. She was the chatterer, he was the listener. She was slight of frame making him look like her protector. Together they were perfect for each other and looked like they loved to laugh. When the cows finally allowed us passage we decided to drive in convoy to Applecross as wild camping was on all our minds.

We found a remarkable spot on a western cliff just before the village knowing that the sun would set in front of us and be a most perfect backdrop for our conversation, drinks and food. They made a big curry for all of us and by the time a large red sun touched the ocean we were already chatting like old friends.

In the morning, Kenny's eyes lit up whilst my heart sank as we met our first bite of midges. Maybe the time had come to unpack the dreaded black head net that made me look like a gothic bride. But instead, with incense sticks being wafted around and citronella candles left burning by the vans we took our cups of tea and followed an untrodden path down through the ferns to reach a midge free rocky beach. The crystal-clear chilly waters of The Inner Sound glimmering in the morning sunshine slapped the rocks as the low sun cast our elongated shadows. Yep, this was Scotland at its best. We drank our morning cuppas overlooking the Isles of Rona, Raasay and Skye. We all felt like we had been transported to another country. Best of all, by the time we had returned to the vans the midges had moved on. Never to be seen again! Kenny sulked in the corner of the van.

It was a lovely hot morning so I jumped on the bike for my second ride and rode around the deserted coastline, past the gallery on the hill and down every road that ended with an End of the Road sign. Back in the village I rewarded myself with half a dozen oysters and a pint of Scottish brewed Hoppy 1st Birthday back at the Applecross Inn.

When I got back to our wild camping spot, two of us found a waterfall to wash in so we splashed about in that for a while, slipping on the wet stones and squealing at its freezing torrents. It's not often you can relive such childhood memories and feel free enough to be childlike again. Whilst we had been splashing around in the waterfall, her husband had managed to re-wire the electrics from my leisure battery to my fridge which had been playing up for a while. So sweet of him. In the magic hour of the sun setting, we built a fire, cooked dinner, toasted marshmallows and chatted till the stars shone.

The lovely thing about meeting new people on the road is that you connect in a different way. No history, no shared memories, just new stories, new points of view, new ideas, new laughter. You can enjoy an unconditional friendship knowing that you'll be moving on soon and may never see each other again. But this time, collectively, we decided to stay together for another day here. Why leave paradise?

TWELVE

17th July: HebCelt Heaven

PHOTO REFS G3 – I2

We enjoyed another night in Applecross and then drove together up the coast to find another remote spot to wild camp for our final night together. We spent the day tinkering and pottering and walking. It had been such a lovely and unexpected hang out. When we did finally part ways we all got the feeling that we would see each other again so it wasn't too hard saying goodbye. They did indeed come to stay with me in London a couple of months after we returned.

But I also knew that another Celtic adventure was about to happen on a remote Isle, so closing one fun chapter to move on to an unknown chapter was what this journey was all about...

As I drove away from heavenly Applecross I played *I Can See Clearly Now* by Johnny Nash. In 1988 the track was used in a Nescafé ad. A girl in her twenties drives in her white VW Beetle and stops on the edge of a cliff overlooking the sea, clearly upset about something (one can only assume it was man troubles!). She lifts her coat to reveal a jar of Nescafé in her bag. She rummages around in the glove box to luckily reveal an element that plugs into the cigarette lighter. With a steaming black coffee in hand she sits on her bonnet and you just know that the world will be a better place without him. '*Make a fresh start*' was the strap line. I come from the land of advertising and, although it's a great looking ad it's not the most effective piece of advertising for me. I bought the VW Beetle rather than becoming a Nescafé drinker. It was my first car. He was white and called Sebastian. I later found out that I am allergic to coffee, so Nescafé was never on my shopping list but the ad most definitely kicked off my love, and life long relationship, with V-Dubs.

I carried on heading north to the lovely port town of Ullapool, which also ended up as the furthest North I ventured. I would have loved to have had more time to travel further up the west and north coasts as I'd heard that *the best pies ever* were in Lochinvar and *the best beach ever* was Achmelvich Bay but, due to Charlie's inability to move at speed, I just didn't get the chance to see them. Next time for sure...

Instead, the pipes and fiddles of HebCelt music festival in Stornaway on the Isle of Lewis were calling me. One more sleep and I'd be in the Outer Hebrides! I find any new experience thoroughly exciting so I could hardly contain myself at the thought of boarding my first of many sea-faring voyages - in a van with a cat! I only spent a night in Ullapool but I could have stayed longer. The seafront housed traditional pubs all offering live music and I found the most delicious hot giant garlic crab claws at the Seafood Shak, recommended by a neighbour back home, which were bigger and better than I could have expected. I live for expectations being exceeded.

And HebCelt 2019 was everything I wanted it to be, and more. It was sold out and the campsites were a patchwork of colourful tents. All the vintage VW campers were parked together in the overspill fields so immediately a new community of V-Dubbers was formed and new friends made. My main festival buddies were a father and adult son duo who had taken turns driving through the night from Birmingham to get there.

It was just the right sized festival for me with around 15,000 people over three days honouring all things with Celtic roots. Fantastically different bands like Face the West who grew up on the island and formed 20 years ago when they were 15 in order to avoid as much schooling as possible. Such energy and fun on stage. Another local band called Peat & Diesel had become an unexpected online phenomenon, adored by a younger crowd, who would go absolutely nuts when they played live. To the surprise of the oldies these kids, high on the *craic*, required crowd control from the local police, fire department and the coast guard! Luckily, only fun was had and no fights ensued, no onshore fires needed extinguishing and no offshore souls needed saving.

Awkward Family Portraits took me back to my teenage. They were a brilliant Glaswegian skiffle, rock-a-billy band complete with quiffs, slicked back hair and a double bass; JigJam were a high energy Irish bluegrass quartet and Elephant Sessions, who should have headlined, were an explosion of Celtic trad, funk and electronica. The music had been brilliant, the craft beer was perfect, the local gin was delicious, the crowds had danced and cheered and the sun shone. Boom!

Three days later the festival was over so I headed out on the Sunday morning to drive down to Harris but, before I went, I made a wee detour. Let it be said that I am not a church goer, the convent put me off that, but I decided to attend the Stornoway Free Church service as I had heard that they would be singing Gaelic Psalms and I was really interested to experience them. When sung well, they sound like the rolling waves of an ocean on a dark night. Oh and had I mentioned that they were also offering a free breakfast? Food was a definite lure so off I went to find their large, grey Presbyterian church. Utilitarian design at its best.

The decadent triple bacon and egg bap didn't disappoint and was the perfect antidote to a three-day fest. The old girls in the hall who were serving breakfast were absolutely delightful and were thoroughly intrigued and surprisingly supportive as they heard the story of my solo travels and offered me further cups of tea in order to see more pictures of Kenny.

The interior of the church was perfectly symmetrical which suited my disposition. I took a seat in the wooden gallery overlooking the wooden pews below. The sermon was given by an aptly named Reverend Kenneth who also led the Psalms for the congregation to follow. Gaelic Psalms are prayers sung with no music, and the melody is made up on the fly by the Reverend which changes each time they are sung. Rev

Kenny sang the first line and the congregation repeated the lines which would then cross over and merge with the next line. It was mesmerising and meditative. As I could neither read nor sing in Gaelic, I picked up a Bible that I had been given upon arrival.

I guess a Catholic schoolgirl should have been familiar with the Bible but at no point during my education had the nuns asked us to read it. So here I was at 52 reading Genesis for the first time. I knew about God creating the world in six days and resting on the seventh, I knew about Adam and Eve, the Garden of Eden (my mother's initials) and about the serpent, oh and I knew about Joseph and his brothers as our class was chosen to be in the choir in the touring production with Jess Conrad in 1980. But that was about it so I began to read. To be honest, I don't think an 11-year-old would have been ready to comprehend God's reaction to Eve eating the forbidden fruit. For He said unto her:

"I shall give you intense pain in childbearing, you will give birth to your children in pain. Your yearning will be for your husband, and he will dominate you."

Crikey. Not sure that was His kindest nor best decision. I read no further.

The Reverend's sermon was a bit more uplifting as he told a story of a Christian who wore two bags. One on his front and one on his back. During each day he'd place all good things, good deeds and positive thoughts into his front bag and, in the bag on his back, he'd place all negative things and wrong doings that had happened that day. Before he went to bed each night he would take the bag from his back without looking in and tie a knot in it and throw it away, never to be considered again. He'd then unpack the bag from his front and consider all the good things that happened that day. An effective parable but I soon realised I had a better one of my own that I'll share with you later.

After church, as I jumped in the van to drive south to Harris, I received a text from 02 stating that I had already reached my data limit and my 6GB would be refreshed in 20 days! I couldn't survive the rest of the trip without data. How could I have used up so much so quickly? I suddenly realised what I'd done. Before I had set off on my adventure I had thought long and hard about how to post my journey on social media. I'm not into posting my life through these channels but I guessed my family and friends would be interested in how I was getting on. I decided to download an app called *Relive* to track my journey and post a few words and photos along the way. *Relive* tracks your GPS and then creates a cute little animation to music of a satellite map of you moving from A to B including elevation, speed and any photos you take along the way. It's brilliant! A little white dot traverses rapidly showing every hairpin bend, loch and hill that you drive through and, if you replace the white dot with my little blue house on wheels, you're pretty much travelling with me.

Lovely as they were, after about six posts I realised that it was that, plus Google maps guiding me north, that was burning through data faster than Charlie could ever dream of moving. In a panic I immediately bought the biggest bundle I was 'allowed' which would sate me for a while but would definitely not get me to my renewal date. "*Why don't you just use Wi-Fi?*" I can hear you say. Well, there is not an abundance of Wi-Fi cafés in the Outer Hebrides and whenever I stopped at a café or a bar the first thing I'd ask was if they had Wi-Fi. From the air of desperation in my voice and my widened eyes it always felt like I was asking for a methadone hit and they looked at me like I was a junkie! Which I was! I needed data! I didn't think I could function without it!

At that moment I realised the silver lining hiding in this digital cloud. Switching off the data meant switching off the noise. "*Hallelujah,*" I shouted in true atheist style. Bring on more uninterrupted silence.

My data rationing began at once as I headed out of Stornoway sans SatNav. I was now using a map, printed on paper, in a book, called an Atlas. The ultimate offline tool. Although every now and then I'd catch myself trying to enlarge the image with two fingers. For a fraction of a second I couldn't understand why it wasn't getting any bigger, then I realised was an idiot. The open Atlas on the passenger seat also didn't stop me getting lost but it didn't really matter as part of the fun of a road trip was now getting lost and finding the unknown – although a friend of mine had also reminded me that not all who wander are lost, and that definitely rang true.

THIRTEEN

21st July: Wild, wild camping in the wild, wild west

PHOTO REFS D1 – K5

I wanted to investigate the west coast and spend another night on Lewis before heading south.

My pencil cross on my map was taking me to Kneep, another white-sanded expanse on the west coast of Lewis, but along the way I found an absolutely beautiful spot on a remote cliff, in a place called Cliff, overlooking a huge stretch of deserted white sand with aquamarine water. It looked amazing even in the rain which had just started to fall. I parked Charlie up on the cliff with two large picnic table benches between us and the cliff edge as my wind break. I spotted a walled graveyard to my right, the lucky residents had a dead nice view for eternity. It hadn't been a long drive but I was tired post festival so I cooked dinner washed down with a couple of locally brewed beers and headed for bed early, not realising I was about to push the boundaries of wild camping a bit too far...

It certainly wasn't bedtime for the elements as the wind gathered speed and the thick rain continued to pour. Their nocturnal energies seemed to build exponentially into a frenzy throughout the night. The van was now being blown around so much that it felt like six burly men were outside rocking it. This went on for eight hours.

The mind can really play tricks when you know you are stranded alone in the pitch black... with a cemetery 100 yards away. I daren't even look through the curtains just in case it wasn't the wind rocking Charlie, so I sat with my 'attitude adjuster' in hand ready to fight anything that my imagination allowed me to conjure up.

Scotland has a zero tolerance policy on drinking and driving and as I'd had a couple of beers, I knew I wouldn't be allowed to drive to a safer place. I just had to hunker down with Kenny as protection.

This was the first time I had actually wished for someone else to be with me, just so I could say "*Is this OK? Are we OK?*" as I certainly didn't feel OK. The logical side of my brain was confident enough that the bolted down picnic tables would be our bolster and stop us from plummeting into the sea below. But I still had visions of Charlie being rocked further and further into the ground rendering me rooted in the mud and unable to move in the morning. Kenny was none the wiser and enjoyed his usual nocturnal activities as much as the wind and rain so all I could do was duck when Kenny launched himself at me at full speed. I tried to distract myself by watching Season 2 of Killing Eve on my iPad, though upon reflection I should have chosen a lighter box set.

I must have finally dozed off as the iPad was out of juice as the morning came. It was reassuring that the van was no longer being thrown around but as I slowly woke I could hear strange knocking and banging sounds from all around the van. Kenny peered through the curtains and by watching his head dart about I knew he was looking at something. "*Oh God, now what?!*" I tentatively peered through the curtains to reveal a flock sheep surrounding the van using Charlie as their wind breaker as they grazed the wet grass around him. Their horns knocking the van had been my wake-up call.

Maybe wild camping on such a remote high plateau in gale force winds and torrential rain next to dead people wasn't such a good idea after all. Luckily Charlie wasn't stuck in the mud and I headed off immediately to Harris, tired and hungry.

My exit track was *Orphan Girl* by Gillian Welsh. And I had felt like a little abandoned orphan that morning. I've learnt to rise above those lonely feelings though and, as singing lifts the soul, I sang along in harmony on repeat.

On my way out, I drove past an eight-foot wooden sculpture of one of the Lewis Chessmen. These chess pieces recently hit the press when one of the missing Medieval warders had been found in a drawer and was sold at Sotheby's for an astonishing £735k! My huge wooden King had a mighty presence and as I approached him I thanked him for protecting me last night.

•

The Isle of Harris is at the southern tip of the Isle of Lewis and both isles are joined which meant two things. One, I didn't need to get a ferry and two, it made no sense to call them both isles.

Anyway, I had really been looking forward to my visit to Harris for three reasons. Gin, Harris Tweed and the Coffin Road.

The distillery itself was an impressive utilitarian building that looked more like a Presbyterian church than a house of gin, though I guess if you drink too much you'll still end up on your knees singing out of tune. I didn't take the gin tour but headed straight for the shop instead and came out with an iconic bottle of Harris Gin infused with sugar kelp, two matching glasses and a honeysuckle face balm. Delighted with my purchases and with my spirits well and truly lifted it was time to buy a little something for Kenny. My little Scottish steam punk looked very dashing indeed in his pink and purple Harris Tweed collar. I'm not quite sure he agreed... in fact I think it's the first time he ever pulled an expression!

Coffin Road, the Golden Road and the Sleeping Lady Rock surrounded my next destination. Lickisto campsite. Amazingly, I was on to my second book and was now thoroughly enjoying reading. It was another Peter May called *Coffin Road*, a murder mystery in which he describes this area with such atmospheric darkness and beauty I was looking forward to experiencing it for myself – though I hoped that the body count would be kept to a minimum during my visit.

Some campsites are just fields to park in and some campsites are just magical. Lickisto is the latter. Each camping spot had been surrounded by tall bamboos and trees so everyone felt totally secluded. The land contained two original backhouses now converted with all their rustic charm to be used as communal areas for cooking, washing, chatting and playing music. These backhouses brought everyone together and it felt like a mini temporary community.

That day I had jumped on the bike again for my third ride. These remote Scottish roads are perfect to ride on. No vehicles, traffic lights, no interruptions, just a mix of gently undulating and challenging hills to enjoy placed amongst more dramatic unique scenery. The skies were dark and the roads were black. The rocky land was peppered with tiny lochs, called lochans, with wild water lilies floating on their mirrored surface. I felt like the only survivor in an apocalyptic heaven.

It was a comfortable 25-mile ride via The Golden Road that twisted and turned through its lunar-like landscape with an out-of-this-world head wind that never gave up. It certainly did feel like a particular trait of riding these isles, regardless of your direction: you battle a headwind.

The guy who ran the campsite had lived one hell of a life and now enjoyed the sanctuary of living alone in the third blackhouse right in the middle of his campsite. On my last day, he invited me over for dinner. I knew instantly that this invitation was genuine so nothing untoward even crossed my mind. He had so many fantastic stories to tell and we whiled away the hours sharing anecdotes over a couple of bottles of wine with nice juicy steaks cooked on the outside grill.

Whether someone is travelling in a van or has chosen a remote isle to start again, this life of 'less is more' has clearly brought out a truer, kinder spirit in everyone I have met. It is so refreshing and heartening to witness. And for the ones I have met who are alone, they project no sense of loneliness. They seem to have reconciled their past and continue to grow from this quieter life. It's very encouraging and inspiring to see, though it started making me feel rather anxious about returning home to a busy, smelly, unfriendly London.

I had another revelation as I headed back to the van after a morning's walk through the bamboos when I vaguely overhead someone say that Boris Johnson was our new Prime Minister. *Oh God.* It felt like I had just been pulled from a dream into a nightmare and my heart sank. I'd managed to not listen to the news for 17 days and I suddenly realised how liberating it had been not following every twist and turn of our political reality show. Some of my friends and colleagues who delight in discussing politics on a Friday night have chided me for not joining in with their political discussions but I still refuse to engage, especially with a glass of chilled white in hand.

Since editing this chapter, our country has now left Europe and a deadly virus has taken over and the world is in lockdown. By the time you read this God only knows what state we'll be in. Pick a Hollywood disaster movie and it could be that, though I hoped that Hollywood would write a better ending than the one we had in store...

I wished my Dad was still alive. He had his finger on the current affairs pulse and I would insist on him giving me non-biased evaluations of politics and history in laymen's terms. As a Tory he could never fathom where I had got my Socialist tendencies from, but to be honest, as I've never enjoyed discussing politics and chose to keep my opinions to myself. Actions speak louder than words. But he would have been fascinated by the utter craziness of 2019 and 2020.

FOURTEEN

A death, an angel and a visitation

Dad died on 14th December 2014 at the age of 77. Over the last couple of decades he had become my friend, my phone-a-friend, my go-to for support and was still the only man who ever knew how to temper me. He was a font of knowledge. His email address was *FABnorth@yahoo.com* which stood for Fatherly Advice Bureau, though his advice was sought by all, not just his daughters.

I'm not sure if this is a bit odd but I still have 17 messages from him on my landline answer phone that I listen to from time to time. In fact, I've just played them all back now. I find it rather comforting to hear such a familiar voice after so long. One of his messages made me smile again. *"Old age isn't good for one's health,"* he said, ruminating on his own ageing process.

He was always a fit and healthy man and had only been to the doctor once in his life when he broke his arm at the age of 15. Even then he only went to hospital after completing his maths exam, which he passed. At school, Dad was captain of the running team and later went on to run four marathons so, along with his brilliant mind, his mobility was everything to him.

At 74 he developed Peripheral Neuropathy, which meant that the nerves going from his brain and spinal cord to his hands and feet became damaged and, even though there was nothing physically wrong with his peripheries, his brain believed there was. Because of this he lost his balance and had to shuffle around using a Zimmer. He also wore two pairs of thick thermal gloves at all times as his hands felt freezing cold, even though they weren't, and if he touched paper he felt like his hands were on fire.

The closest thing I can imagine is when you come home from the bitter cold and you try to get your keys out of your bag to unlock the door but your fingers are so cold they don't work and hurt like hell. You fumble around on the wrong side of the door, in the cold, in pain, when there's nothing actually wrong with you. I think it felt a bit like that, but all time.

"I can handle losing my mobility but the minute I lose my marbles will you kill me?" he eventually said to me, and he meant it. We had many conversations on how to 'bump him off' but sadly for him, I wasn't quite prepared to go to prison for murdering my father so he died in the worse place possible for him. In hospital. How I wish I could have killed him in a nicer way so his final moments on this earth were less stressful than a bunch of medics pounding at his chest trying to resuscitate him regardless of his final wishes of Do Not Resuscitate. The thought of that still brings tears to my eyes.

My sister and I were brought up in a pretty strict household. Dad was the disciplinarian and Mum showered us with love. She brought laughter, positivity and creativity into our lives and never told us off. Though if we were ever naughty in public then a firm squeeze of our hand and a 'look' from her was enough to nip any bad behaviour in the bud. She was the one that planned fun weekend trips. Dad was the one who would always say there'd be nowhere to park.

From small children to young adults he was a pretty distant and unaffectionate father to us. I think we heard him laugh once. When my sister and I were young children we'd wait in the kitchen at six o'clock every night knowing Dad was about to drive around the corner from work. We'd run downstairs to greet him, and each time we'd be greeted with *"Not now girls, I'm tired and need a cup of tea."* We'd make him that cup of tea and wait in the playroom for him to come to play with us but he never did.

What he did do was reading before bedtime. Not fun reading though.

Not him reading stories with funny voices to make us laugh, Mum would do that brilliantly (*Little Spook* was our favourite). It was us having to read to him as homework. My sister loved reading more than life itself and would want to read the whole book but he'd only let her read about five pages, so she would go to bed frustrated. I hated reading more than life itself so I would negotiate to read as few pages as possible but I still had to read about five pages. I would go to bed upset. Not the best Dad skills but, to be fair, he had had a very odd childhood himself.

He was Ukrainian-Austrian, born Jewish but brought up Catholic. During the war he was sent away to a convent in Ilfracombe where the nuns would beat him and lock him in a cupboard. His teen years were spent at Downside, a Catholic boarding school and the home of Benedictine culture. In keeping with the Tom Brown's Schooldays era, my Dad's school practiced 'fagging', a system where younger boys were required to act as servants and perform 'personal duties' for the older boys. In reality, fagging meant being 'regularly buggered' by the six formers from the age of 11 upwards.

Dad had been a very pretty little boy so fell victim to this behaviour for years. He told me this brutal fact at a family party when he and I were sitting outside in the garden. His delivery was so matter of fact he could have been saying "*Fancy a slice of cake?*" How was an awkward teenage daughter meant to react to a statement like that from her father? I had no idea what to say.

He filled the silence by telling me that when he got to sixth form he and his classmates announced that the days of fagging at Downside were over. I'm so proud that at that age he fought the fight and won, but it's beyond horrific to think what happened to him. I don't know how he managed to reconcile or recover from that abuse. To be honest I don't think he ever did. That certainly explains his distance and inability to show love.

After about 30 years of marriage Mum and Dad decided to split up and live in different houses. Dad stayed in our family home in Manchester and Mum moved into a house in Richmond that had been left to her by her first husband's mother. Her first husband had been killed in a car crash during their first year of marriage, which obviously devastated Mum and his mother. But when Mum eventually re-married, her first mother-in-law took to Dad like her son and became a third grandmother to me and my sister. It was truly amazing.

So when Mum had finally had enough of Dad's difficult ways and dour outlook on life it was in the Richmond house that she sought solace. They didn't separate to be with anyone else, she just needed space away from him. And I totally understood and supported her decision. Dad just needed to lighten up and realise what a great family he had.

I think the time alone made him reflect as, out of the blue, he called me and apologised for not being a loving father. He regretted not being affectionate towards us and hoped that we could start again. The power of receiving an apology from someone who had never apologised before was palpable and, with that, our relationship dramatically changed. I can honestly say that he became a friend. My own inability to apologise comes directly from him. Note to self... I must apologise more. It kinda works!

I had always had such a fantastic relationship with my Mum it was now so comforting to have the final piece of the parenting puzzle in place. I just hoped that it wasn't too late for my now separated parents.

My Mum is adorable and I call her Little Mums. She is the eldest of seven sisters with one older and two younger brothers. From looking at old family photos I always thought that she looked like a dark haired Marilyn Monroe. She was a right beauty. Born in Foochow (Fuzhou), China in 1929 she had a privileged start to life, living there for nine years and going to a Mickey Mouse school, as she called it, as all they did was colour in. She can still sing *It's A Long Way To Tipperary* in some form of Chinese dialect!

She was an amazing artist and her sketch books were filled with facsimiles of her sisters in pencil, gentle water colours of landscapes and, later, perfectly penned outlines of me and my sister. Sadly, she was never allowed to pursue her creative ambitions and I often wonder how different her life would have been if she had been given the freedom to do so. Maybe that's why she gave us such creative freedom.

We had a playroom at home full of Galt toys, modelling clay, puppets, paints and crayons and computer paper – those perforated reams of paper with sprocket holes down both sides and pale green lines on the back that Dad had commandeered from work. We'd bake cakes and biscuits and design and make clothes together. As a teenager we would shop and lunch for hours and laugh loudly with tears in our eyes. With my rose tinted glasses on I can't even remember having an argument with her.

That is why, even though she is still alive, I miss her so much.

During Mum and Dad's split, a trilogy of terrible events happened which ended with an unexpected love story. First of all, Mum tripped on a paving stone outside the Richmond house and fell on her face breaking a couple of fingers and scarring her mouth. No sooner had she recovered from that she was diagnosed with mild Alzheimer's. She was put on pills to stabilise its development which meant that she was still able to live on her own. Finally, Mum got breast cancer and had a mastectomy. I say this final part in one short sentence as she was so stoic we hardly even noticed it had happened. She is in fact the most stoic person I have ever met.

These run of events were enough for Dad to insist that he looked after her properly and they decided to live together again, alternating between the two houses. Mum made a full recovery from the first and third disasters but it was only when they'd got back together that we realised that there was an unexpected positive side to Alzheimer's. She couldn't remember what a twat my Dad had been! All of a sudden, she was *"Oh, look at your lovely blue eyes!"* giving him a hug, and *"You're so handsome!"* taking his hand and saying *"What would I do without you?"*

Dad obviously lapped up the compliments but with the 'look' I had learnt from Mum I'd say to him *"You're so bloody lucky! Don't fuck this up!"* He understood my 'look' and he didn't fuck it up. He became the most wonderful, supportive and protective husband he could be. My heart would melt as I watched them toddle off hand in hand. Over the next couple years they were inseparable, like two little Stickle Bricks. As Dad lost his mobility Mum was there to run around after him and as Mum's memory grew worse Dad was there to remember.

·

In the five weeks leading up to Dad's death, I had been up in Manchester looking after both my parents. It all began when I received a call at home at about 3am from a paramedic in my parents' house saying that he had just, literally, picked up Dad off the floor and was about to take him to hospital after a collapse. But because Dad was Mum's carer they couldn't leave her at home alone so they asked if I could come to the hospital to pick her up. I explained that I lived in London but would get there as soon as I could. I promptly jumped in the car and drove 200 miles north to meet them at the hospital. I was up there for five weeks.

When I arrived at Stepping Hill Hospital, the very same hospital where a rogue nurse had been recently poisoning and killing patients by lethal injection – not the most comforting medical environment to find your parents – I found Mum tucked up comfortably in a hospital bed whilst Dad was still waiting in a chair in the corridor!

"*What on earth are you doing in a bed Mum, there's nothing wrong with you?!*" I had to laugh at the absurdity.

"*Oh I don't know,*" she said laughing and sipping her tea, "*but everyone's being very nice to me here!*"

I got her dressed, waited several hours till Dad got settled in to a proper bed in a ward and, as a treat, took her to lunch at our local chippy. We ate in, as we had done on special occasions when we were kids, and on the drive home she asked:

"*What are we going to eat for lunch?*"

I could only laugh. "*But you've just eaten your body weight in fish, chips, mushy peas, gravy, bread'n'butter and ice cream! Are you hungry?"*

She laughed loudly and said *"Oh, I don't know!"* And with that I suddenly realised the level of care Mum needed. Thankfully, another silver lining to Mum's condition was that she lost her memory with great humour so we laughed a lot and she wiped away her tears with her Whittaker's Chippy napkin.

With no clear diagnosis, Dad was discharged, re-admitted, discharged with this pattern continuing on repeat for several weeks. When Dad had been at home for a few days I popped out one afternoon and returned with bags filled with lever-arch files, coloured dividers and post-its.

"What have you got there?" Dad asked intrigued.

"Oh, I've got a game for us to play this afternoon, and Mum can join in too..." I replied.

Not one for games at the best of times Dad looked a bit confused. *"Hmmm, what is it?"*

"It's called Filing All Your Crap Into One Place So I Know Where It All Is When You're Gone!"

Dad gave me the same look that I used to give him when he used to make me read as a child. Ha! Revenge!

As a family, we had never shied away from talking about death so we all knew the purpose of this game. Dad had promised for years to put everything together on a pen drive for me to make it easier when he was gone, but to no avail, so the three of us spent the rest of the afternoon going through huge piles of disorderly paperwork. Dad's job was to lift up every sheet and tell me what it was. My job was to hole punch and file accordingly. Mum was in charge of recycling. Several hours later a final cup of tea and slice of cake was reward for seeing a colourful display of folders lined up on the dining room table filled to the brim with alphabetised sections that made us all smile.

We even found the historic documents and items that we had only heard existed. One document giving my Austrian great-grandparents alien rights to live in the UK, signed in 1910 by Winston Churchill when he was Home Secretary. And a wax seal of the *de Nordwall* coat of arms which I now have tattooed on my right forearm! Dad would turn in his grave if he knew I'd been inked and I have to pretend to Mum that I've drawn it on with biro!

My first tattoo was the word PAX on my right wrist that was done four days after Dad died. A couple of decades prior to this, I had cunningly swapped my first old PC laptop with the family Olivetti Valentine typewriter, the one you'll find in the design museum. I had enthusiastically suggested to Dad that he could finally join the digital age and trawl the internet and even have an email address. It took a while to convince him as he was still a fan of going to the library and writing letters. But my new found persuasive skills worked. The swap was made and he completely fell in love with his new technology and became a computer wizard.

With his new email set up he'd sign off his emails to me with –

Lots of love from MA x and PA x

The kiss after each name soon became MAX and PAX so, with PAX meaning *peace* in Latin, it was the perfect choice for my first tattoo. When Mum goes I'll have MAX inked on my left wrist, which will always reassure me that they will be both be resting in *maximum peace* together.

•

On Dad's repeated stays in hospital I kept Mum tucked under my wing whilst I felt powerless witnessing my Dad shrink and fade from the strong man I knew to a skeletal shadow of my father. The biggest challenge was how to deal with the awkward role reversal for Dad morphing from parent to child and, for me, from child to parent without revealing it on our faces. There are some things you just don't want to see and can't unsee once seen. But in true de Nordwall style, we just got on with it.

A couple of days before Dad died he was back in hospital. In the early hours of the morning I was lying in bed when I heard what I can only describe as a wild animal in the house. I sat bolt up in bed quickly working out how to extract a rogue urban fox but it turned out to be Mum having a seizure. Her hands were tightly clenched and her body was stiffened. I tried to wake he up but couldn't get her round so I called 999. After some time, the paramedic was able to get her conscious and she was then admitted to the same hospital as Dad, though in the adjoining ward. Visiting times felt like an episode of Carry On Parents with me trotting from one bed to another carrying messages to and from my parents as both were too ill to be moved out of their beds to see each other. I still find it extraordinary how we could still find humour during these disturbing times and the nurses would sometimes have to ask us to keep the noise down from laughing too loudly.

The doctors and I were constantly conjuring up more medical remedies to get Dad back on his feet, albeit slightly wobbly ones, but I always thought he'd recover. As a family who like to be prepared, it was agreed for me to be Executor of his Will and I now held Power of Attorney for his, and Mum's, health and wealth. From his hospital bed Dad would watch me in animated discussions with the medics and I think he felt comfort in that. He could see me managing his affairs and, for once, someone was fighting for him. In retrospect, I think he made his decision then that there was no more for him to do, and thus, it was time for him to let go.

Dad died on the Sunday without seeing Mum for one last time.

I got the call at 6am from the hospital asking me to come in as Dad was not well. They recommended I got a taxi. I didn't realise then but this meant that he had already died. As I approached the double doors to his ward I was spotted by the on-duty nurse mouthing *"She's here,"* to another nurse. I was taken into an uncomfortably bright side room and was told the news and everything started to slow down.

I wasn't ready for him to go. I thought they'd both be coming home. I didn't know how to react. I felt numb and buried my face in my scarf unable to cry. I felt like I was falling backwards down a deep dark well with no one to catch me. I tried to hold on to the light at the top of the well. They brought me milky tea (I hate milky tea) and I sat alone in the brightness for a while without a thought.

Another nurse walked past the door, saw me out of the corner of her eye, turned around and came into the room. I can still remember every detail of her. I'm used to spotting details, patterns and irregularities in life but as I looked at her I couldn't find anything out of place. I felt instantly at ease with her. She calmly said *"I know you're not OK but I just wanted to see how you are."*

"Not OK," I replied.

"That's understandable," she said and sat down on the chair next to me. *"Good,"* I thought. I felt reassured that I was OK not to feel OK and yet not know what to feel.

"Would you like to see your Dad?"

"NO!" I said with eyes widened in a cracked voice. I'd never seen a dead body and didn't want my father's to be my first one.

"I think you should," she said in very matter of fact way. *"It's important for you to see that your father has died. It won't take away from him being your father but it will make it easier for you to move forward. It's important to physically say goodbye."*

It seemed logical enough. It was like talking to Dad. As she spoke I remember noticing her skin was particularly glowing and then looking at her hairline thinking that she'd managed to tie her hair back just right. No stray hairs sticking out and nothing scraped back too tightly. Nice and symmetrical. Very comforting.

I agreed and stood up. She asked me if I'd like to take her hand. I did. We walked hand in hand to a room at the end of the corridor. As soon as I entered I saw that my Dad's mouth was open and I didn't like it. I stopped immediately, turned to her and asked her if she could close his mouth. Without any pause she said no and told me to go in. Without debate I went in.

There's nothing more surreal. It's impossible to get your head around. I guess that's why such a logical approach was the only one to take, especially for me. I told her that he once was a strong athlete who ran marathons. I hesitated putting my hand on his head and looked at her. She told me that it was OK. That he was still my father. I touched his head and said a silent goodbye.

We walked back to the bright room where we first met and I took a seat. I looked up to say thank you but she had gone. I stood up to look down the corridor but she wasn't there either. I stopped. I sat down again. Did that actually happen? Now, I see myself as a logical person, not into spirits or guides, but I still have no idea if she actually existed. Whoever, or whatever, she was I can still remember every detail vividly and I thank her with eyes raised to the heavens for the perfectly practical manner in which I got to say goodbye to Dad.

Spiritual has never been a word that I've been comfortable with but, the following morning another *unusual* thing happened that makes me question my life, the universe and everything.

Little Mums was still in hospital and wasn't going to be discharged for another few days. I'd broken the news about Dad to my sister and aunt on the phone, who both lived in London and both jumped on a train immediately up to Manchester. Together we decided not to tell Mum about Dad until she was back in the comfort of her own home and we requested that all the medical staff agreed not to mention it either.

The next morning we visited Mum. When we got to the hospital we found her already dressed, sitting peacefully in the chair beside her bed. She had packed her belongings in her bag and folded all her linen on the bed into neat piles. The nurses didn't know why she had done this either. We asked her what she was doing and she said calmly that Dad had come to see her the night before and told her that she was going to go down to London on the train and needed to get ready. So she was getting ready.

"*In a dream?*" we asked.

She laughed and said no. "*He came to see me last night and told me to pack my bag.*"

We managed to cajole her to unpack and get back into bed saying that she needed to stay here for a couple more days but then she'd go home.

The funny thing was that Mum had never got the train down to London before as Dad had always driven everywhere. But as it turned out, a couple of weeks later, Mum did end up catching the train down to London to stay with her sister whilst we worked out where she would live on a permanent basis. Once again, Dad was right!

•

Dad was a Humanist. Someone who believes that there is no after life, Heaven or Hell and that your time on this earth should be used as effectively as possible. I'd rather liked the idea that you only get one go at life. You're a one hit wonder and, in that time, you need to be the best person you can be and your memory is based on the legacy you leave through the people you have affected. But now I'm not quite sure what I believe as both these experiences have made me question my understanding of our time on earth. Does our spirit live on after our life? Are we able to visit people after death? Was that nurse an angel?

Spirits and angels aside, I decided to make more of a difference on this earth.

Four days after Dad died I attended my cousins funeral back in London. She was a year older than me, a model, a stand-up comedian with a fabulous husband and two wonderful boys. She died of cancer. Too tragic. We sang my favourite hymn, *How Great Thou Art*, which brought tears to my eyes. The last time I had sung this was at my Godmother's funeral and I was standing next to Dad. I'd never heard him sing before and we found a funny moment together when we realised I was singing an octave below him. Today there were no smiles.

FIFTEEN

Ashes and dust

Like father like daughter, Dad planned ahead so it was pretty obvious that all his funeral arrangements had already been made and paid for. When I met the funeral director, who Dad had chosen at random, he certainly didn't meet any of my expectations of a man in that role. With the bluest of eyes, he was the image of Paul Hollywood, wore a 1920s gangster style three-piece suit and drove a Hummer hearse. How the hell had Dad found this dude? But this dude was definitely in the right job as he was, without doubt, the calmest, most empathetic man I had ever met.

I called him from the hospital the day Dad died overwhelmed by confusion and sadness (grief hadn't begun to kick in yet), whilst also trying to put my producer's hat on and work out what had to be done next. As Executor to Dad's Will, and sole holder of Lasting Power of Attorney for Mum, there seemed to be a million things to consider and to put into action but I had no idea where to start. There's no Dummies Guide to Funerals and it's not the kind of thing you ask your friends.

We were cremating Dad in Manchester and his ashes would be interred in our family plot in Richmond so that was two sets of funerals and wakes to arrange. I had only just recovered from clearing out the Richmond house on my own when Dad had first fallen in Manchester so I wasn't looking forward to the emotional distress of another house clearance. But as I stood in the hospital corridor, the funeral director gave me the best advice I have ever been given.

"You just need to do one thing a day. Work out what that one thing is, and do it. Then stop." His voice and tone was clear, gentle but firm.

One thing a day?! How on earth could I get everything done in time? Already my list of things to do was too long and logic said that one thing a day wouldn't get all that done in time even for the first funeral? But he was right. I did just do one thing a day and somehow everything fell into place.

In the lead up to the funeral he asked me questions I had never considered.

"*What would your Dad like to wear in his coffin?*" was one of the first heart stopping questions that took me completely off guard.

"*Eh?*" I replied, hoping he hadn't just asked me what my Dad would like to wear in his coffin.

"*Well, he's still in his hospital gown so if you'd like him to wear something else then you'll need to send it over and we can dress him. What would he normally wear?*" he replied.

"*Oh, I-I hadn't thought of that.*"

"*Well that's why I'm here.*" he replied calmly.

I paused for thought. "*Well, erm, let me have a think...*" Another pause. It dawned on me that he'd lost so much weight that none of his trousers would fit anymore.

"*Do you think he needs to wear a belt?*" I asked. "*But I guess he's not standing up so maybe not. But then again he always wore a belt so maybe I should bring a belt.*"

"*Good idea, bring the belt.*" he said.

"*What about shoes?*" it started to feel like a conversation from a black comedy.

"*It's up to you.*"

"*Well, I think if it was me, and I was lying down for a while, I'd be more comfortable without shoes, but I think he should wear socks.*" I suggested.

"*Socks it is! Great. If you can you bring them over when you're ready I'll get him dressed.*"

I told Mum the plan and she said she wanted to help choose his outfit with me. She picked out her favourite shirt and I picked his Manchester to Brighton cycling t-shirt to wear underneath the shirt. His usual pair of elephant cords and a pair of socks without holes. Oh, and the belt!

Luckily, one thing I had already ticked off the list was music. A fortnight before he died we were in the kitchen and *Bad Moon Rising* by Creedence Clearwater Revival had come on the radio. Dad started dancing about in his chair with a huge smile on his face. It was the most animated I had seen him, ever, and he must have seen my surprise as he said, *"Your Mum and I saw them live back in the day and we danced all night."* He paused. *"When I'm cremated can this this be my song?"*

"Consider it done!" I said. He was delighted. We played it again.

Mum also jiggled about to the song as Dad rolled into the flames. I hope this doesn't come across too flippantly but it was just the right thing for her to have done. Alzheimer's allows her to live in the moment, without grief from the past or stress from the future, and this clearly brought back a lovely memory for her that she re-lived in that moment. The humanist celebrant told stories from people who had met Dad and shared the impact he had had on their lives and read a piece from me as I was unable to speak. Even their window cleaner had sent in a message about the lovely conversations he and Dad had about the engineering of ladders. Typical Dad. It was unexpected, entertaining and comforting to hear how Dad had connected with so many people.

With the cremation over we needed to keep ticking things off the list and the next item was to clear the Manchester house. It was definitely less traumatic clearing this home than the first one even though this was my only family home and was steeped in my earliest memories. Four years earlier I had cleared the Richmond home alone. Mum and Dad would spend three months at a time in each house so they were both fully functioning houses. It just so happened that they had been in Manchester when Dad first collapsed so they never returned to Richmond again.

•

Clearing a house when both parents are still alive is an unnerving experience. For hours I walked around the house alone, up and down stairs, in and out of every room, around the garden, empty boxes everywhere and a roll of bin bags in hand. I knew I had to just start somewhere but I was happy to procrastinate for a little while longer.

I finally decided that I needed to split the contents of the house into three categories. Things to keep; things to give away to charity; things to chuck.

I started upstairs in the back bedroom. This had always been a special room as it had a tiny staircase in the corner, no wider that two feet with deep steps that led down to the kitchen. This would have been the servant's room, which, for a small two-bedroomed semi was rather a luxury. The room itself was now lined with shelves and each shelf held colourful department store shopping bags (as you know, Mum loved to shop!). I had always been intrigued by the contents of these bags but had resisted the urge to rummage. But now it was a necessity so I prepared myself to find all sorts of goodies inside.

I pulled the first one off the shelf and slowly opened it sitting cross-legged on the floor. Inside was another shopping bag, that contained another bag with tissue paper at the bottom. I took out the light paper and unwrapped... nothing. Eh?! I looked up to the next bag on the shelf and repeated the same thing again and again across a whole wall of bags. This was like a Russian doll version of shopping bags. How odd! What was Mum thinking? It unnerved me that the start to this house clearance, with only one wall cleared, resulted in just a huge pile of rubbish. All the bags went in the recycling bin. *"If it carries on like this I'll be done by the afternoon."* I thought.

But it didn't. It took five days to clear. Five days of stomach churning decisions.

I moved over to the opposite wall to then unearth unopened boxes containing brand new baby toys and clothes. The sudden realisation that Mum must have been buying and saving these for when my sister and I had children was like a stab to the heart. Neither of us produced a grandchild and I suddenly felt heartbroken that I had never given my Mum the opportunity to be a grandmother. She had been such an incredible mother she would have been the best granny ever. This was also validation of why I didn't ask my sister to help. This would have broken her as she has never been able to reconcile not having children.

Luckily, I never mourned about not being a mother but this wasn't the time to dwell on what could have been, or what didn't happen, this was a time to be practical. I filed that emotion away and carried on. I put the new toys and clothes in the charity pile.

If that wasn't hard enough, I then found piles of A4 notebooks filled with pages and pages of Mum's handwritten notes. Mum had beautiful handwriting, that at one time I wanted to turn into a font, so, at first, it was lovely to see so much of it, until I started reading. I realised these were her pre-Alzheimer thoughts on why she had wanted to leave my Dad. I quickly shut the first notebook. It didn't feel right to read my Mum's inner thoughts. Was I meant to read these and decide whether to keep them? Or should I throw them away without consideration? Was there a right thing to do? After pacing for a while, I decided to read them through one eye but I soon realised that it's impossible to unread what you've read even with one eye shut.

It was hard hitting stuff. But now what was I meant to do with them? Mum and Dad were happily back together so why remind her of these darker times. More pacing. With a deep breath I laid them respectfully in another recycling bag.

An unnecessarily huge collection of wine and sherry glasses, with equal piles of linen, joined the toys in the charity pile. Family heirlooms, photographs, jewellery, key pieces of furniture and Mum's paintings were kept and split between the Manchester house and my house for safe keeping.

That was a rough five days and I can still feel the confusing pull of an emotional rollercoaster speeding around a corkscrew of nostalgia and then plummeting into waves of grief. Even though Mum and Dad were still alive at this point I felt like I'd lost something. I suddenly became aware of my parents' mortality and then my mortality but I didn't know what to do with these feelings. However, as with most difficult situations I face, I filed it away and moved on.

•

Before returning to London, after the cremation, I had one final thing to sort. I needed to bring Dad's ashes down to London ready for the interment. My handsome funeral director brought them over to the house in a nice bamboo cask and asked me where I'd like him to put him.

"Is it rude to put him on the kitchen table?" I asked.

"You can put him wherever you like," he said, *"there are no rules."*

I decided to put him at his usual place at the family table, next to my sister's chair, opposite my Mum and diagonal to me. *"He's bloody heavy!"* I said.

"Well it is your Dad!" he said with a slight laugh. *"Do you want to look inside?"*

Yuk. *"NO!"* I screeched. But a laugh came out. *"Is that normal?"*

"Nothing is 'normal', you can do whatever feels right," he replied.

I chose not to peek.

My car was all packed up and I was ready to head off. I then had to work out where to put Dad for the journey. Where does one put one's Dad's ashes? In the boot? On the passenger seat with a seatbelt? In the footwell? I circled the car a couple of times with Dad in my arms hoping my neighbours didn't come out to say goodbye. I decided that the boot was too brutal but he shouldn't be in my view for fear of distraction so I slid him in the footwell behind the front passenger seat, with a copy of *Jonathan Livingston Seagull* wedged on top, and we set off.

I stopped at my usual midway M6 Toll services and treated myself to a naughty Big Mac meal. I was about to devour it when I got the fear that someone might steal the car with Dad in it. My mind started racing about how I could use social media to track him down but then decided it was easier to avoid any potential drama, dramatized on bloody Facebook, and I took my meal to eat in the car.

When I got home, the decision of where to put him returned as I didn't fancy keeping Dad in the house for a week. At this stage I had bought the space above my flat but the renovation hadn't begun so it was being used for storing furniture and anything from the 'things to keep' pile from the Richmond house clearance. The large mirror from above the fireplace was now leaning against a wall with an old ornate fire grate in front. I was too tired to work out if it was macabre or not but I put him in the grate as it seemed the best place for him. He looked quite nice reflected in the mirror so I positioned some candles around him. The night before the interment I lit all the candles and sat having a chat with him as this would be our final night together. In honour of his Austrian heritage I played *Edelweiss* by The Innocence Mission, which was also played at the beginning of his interment.

We had all been astounded at how well Mum was coping with Dad's death, which made us wonder what must it be like for someone with Alzheimer's to grieve. Could she actually remember that Dad had died or was she just wondering where he was? Was she in fact grieving at all or just having to stoically carry on. It certainly wasn't something that I wanted to ask her in case it unfurled something too painful, so all we could do was hope that she wasn't in too much turmoil inside.

We then had the terribly difficult decision of where would Mum now live and who would look after her. We knew she had a good 30 minutes of cognitive thinking before she started going into a looped conversation so we had to present her options to her very carefully. We had decided upon three options in her best interests and it was for me to deliver them to Mum with the aid of clear notes on A3 paper. Option one was for her to stay in the Manchester house with a live-in carer. Option two was the same but in the Richmond house and option three was the one we thought she'd never go for. To move into a care home in London. She considered the options carefully, asked really good astute questions and finally decided upon option three.

She then looked at me and asked what the three pieces of paper on the floor were. We decided to go through the process one more time just in case she wanted a different option, but once again, she chose the home so we felt comfortable that this was the right decision.

A week later Mum moved into a fantastic care home in London, which I know is a rare thing to say. It's a charity residential and nursing home for those who have served in the entertainment industry and it's full of old television and radio personalities, ex tap dancers and jazz pianists. The deep red theatre bar, complete with signed celebrity headshots covering the walls, opens at noon and the old timers wheel in for their pink gins and whisky and gingers on the first stroke of 12. I've already booked my room when I need it!

Of course, Mum had never been an entertainer but it's amazing what the power of a BAFTA, and a poetry performing sister, has. The BAFTA never got me through the door to Hollywood but it jolly well helped getting Mum settled in the best home in London. She says to me on repeat *"I don't know where I am, or what I do every day, but I wake up very happy."* I don't think anyone can ask for more than that.

SIXTEEN

24th July: A whisky-aided ride and a revelation

PHOTO REFS L5 – O5

Thoughts of my family, and memories of my childhood, have filled my head and kept me in good company during my drive. I'm exceedingly lucky to have had such a happy secure childhood. I have been reflecting on how I am most definitely a product of my parents' genes. A very clear 50:50 of both – good and bad! I got Mum's smile, her creativity and stoicism mixed with her super assertiveness (most say bossy!) but definitely got her inability to expect less and accept more. Dad always used to say that the apple doesn't fall far from the tree and I hope that it's true for Mum and me. From Dad, I got his eyes, his logic and dyslexia mixed with his bloody-mindedness and ability to cut off as a protection method.

•

With these thoughts trundling around my head I headed for Skye via my second ferry. So far, no one had recommended anything about Skye to me and I wondered why. All I'd heard was *"Oh it's SO busy."* Although I wondered if it might have seemed busy in comparison to all the silent isles surrounding it. Either way, I made the decision to use Skye as my go through isle and a place to buy all the bits and pieces I needed to continue my journey, like petrol, data cards, batteries, food supplies, wellies, etc.

The ferry from Harris took me to Uig on the northern tip of Skye and I drove south through the functional looking town of Portree where

I managed to buy everything I needed all on one place. Jansvans was a mega hardware store that also had a large café with great Wi-Fi where I sated my online addiction for a couple of hours complete with a supply of tea and scones.

As I continued south, the reviews I'd heard were pretty much spot on. I decided to seek out a waterfall called the Fairy Falls but was discouraged from stopping off as it seemed that the world and his wife were heading there. I'm not a fan of members of the public at the best of times so I wasn't going to share a fairy land with them. The last place that had been recommended, for the vast views alone, was the Cuillin mountain range.

My only option for camping was at the Glen Brittle campsite at the southern tip of Skye, nestled at the base of these humongous mountains. But to get there I had to drive a seven-mile track. At first this track was nice and smooth, but as I approached the campsite in fading light and feathery rain the last mile became pretty challenging. It was steep, rocky and full of potholes so I had to take my time. There were no passing places so we soon became the front car with a line of traffic behind and felt very self-conscious. Like an OAP on a tightrope, Charlie descended with intrepidation. I was pretty terrified too and held on for dear life. We finally arrived to a foggy wet campsite with no view whatsoever. I definitely wasn't feeling Skye.

I shivered, showered, cooked and downed a couple of Skye beers - which proved to be the best thing about Skye thus far. My neighbours on the campsite weren't particularly friendly or chatty so I knew that I wouldn't be making any buddies there, so I curled up with Kenny, pretty much nonplussed by my surroundings.

But then the morning broke and greeted us with the brightest sun and the clearest views of the Cuillins. Once again, I felt miniature looking up at these huge black rocky mountains that reached up to a cloudless sky. Well done Skye, just in the nick of time! The Cuillins are on the Serious Climbers' List of Big and Dramatic Things to Climb and I could already see the hardcore walkers heading out early with their energy bars, bananas and waterproofs.

Well, I thought, if they're doing something adventurous, then so shall I. My fourth bike ride was calling so I grabbed my energy bars and bananas and jumped on the bike. I soon realised that the seven-mile descent the previous day was easy compared to the seven-mile ascent, especially under a blazing sun on a blazing saddle. I panted and chanted my usual mantra when I was faced with a difficult climb "*Fitter for longer, prettier for longer, fitter for longer, prettier for longer.*" It helps to get in a slow rhythmic zone to distract from the leg pain caused by pushing down, pulling up, pushing down, pulling up on repeat. Sometimes I sing Eurythmics' *Sweet Dreams Are Made Of This* as that helps power the legs. I did make a note to self that the way back would be a lot easier.

As soon as I was over the steepest hill I was rewarded with smooth winding roads and crystal-clear views of the mountains and valleys of bright green grass and sparkling rivers. It was like Switzerland on a different planet. Like *The Sound Of Music* meets *The Martian*. I kept jumping on and off the bike to take photos but soon realised that I needed to start taking photos in my head whilst on the move otherwise it would be sundown by the time I got home.

After a couple of hours, I found a perfect half way point. The Talisker distillery. After fish'n'chips at the pub on the waterside I booked myself on to a whisky tour, which of course ended up with a wee dram or two. I learned about mashing and malting, fermenting and distilling. It was like walking around the grown-ups' version of *Charlie and the Chocolate Factory* with huge copper vats that looked like melted caramels and smelt of whisky.

Totally energised for the return trip, I realised that a cheeky whisky is just what you need to get you home. No wonder the cowboys in the big sky country drank so much, it definitely numbs the pain and keeps you in the saddle.

I was knackered by the time I got back to the van so I decided to stay for another night to watch the sun set over the Sea of the Hebrides.

Up bright and early, it was a short drive to the port of Armadale and only a 45-minute sail to Mallaig, back on the mainland. Whilst I was out on deck breathing in the fresh air and feeling burden free, something suddenly clicked into place. An epiphany, worthy of a sermon in a Presbyterian church, and it was all down to Charlie.

You see, when you drive in a vehicle like Charlie, something really interesting starts to happen. As I've said before, 1970s campervans only move at a certain speed. Most of the roads are steep winding single tracks with multiple passing areas and blind summits. They're not an easy drive and you have to keep your wits about you. But after a while I started to notice that, from my position at the wheel, the road ahead was always clear. There was never a car ahead of me. I had the privilege of a perfect view. 20/20 vision. I owned the road. It's like when you're lucky enough to go to the theatre with no one sitting in front of you it feels like the actors are performing just for you.

But then, whilst enjoying this rare experience I'd glance in my rear-view mirror and realise that there was a stream of cars behind me. Oops! Slower vehicles are always encouraged to allow cars to pass and, for that reason, the roads have been built with multiple passing places. Whenever I pulled into these passing zones and let a car go they'd always wave, smile and thank me. Some gave a thumbs up and a little toot to Charlie. No sooner had they passed than they were out of sight and I had the open road all to myself again.

So, at my three-week point, a most cathartic experience happened. With clarity ahead, came clarity of thought. I began to see the empty road as my future. New ideas, dreams, hopes and plans. I had given myself permission to paint my own picture and set my own scene. I started to feel the freedom as I drank in the beauty of these unspoilt vistas. It had a physical effect on me and I could feel something move inside. It felt like falling in love. Without agenda, I was breathing, smiling and enjoying those moments of calm and a sense of hope.

But with this freedom of thought to dream of the future came memories of the past. Thoughts swirled from hopes and dreams to negative ones too, baggage I had been carrying, problems I hadn't solved, people who had wronged me, people I had wronged and, like the cars behind Charlie, I couldn't keep moving forward with so much lingering behind.

So, I decided to 'pin' each individual negative thought or memory onto each car that passed me. I'd lower my window, rotate my arm to indicate for them to pass and as they drove past with smiles on their faces with a wave or a beep they disappeared with my negative thought in tow. They were none the wiser as to which piece of metaphorical baggage or shitty person I had pinned to them but each one disappeared into the distance never to return again.

I then wondered if, by doing this, I was forgiving these people for their wrongdoings, line crossing and unacceptable behaviour? I dwelled on this for a while and finally can came to the conclusion that I wasn't quite ready for that yet! I was happy to forget but not forgive. I'd deal with forgiving them on another day, or maybe on another road trip.

But it did mean, for now, that those two vile women from work who severely crossed the line of professional behaviour were pinned to a crappy little car and were now well and truly out of my head; the director whose extraordinarily cruel behaviour now doesn't even touch the sides; and that idiot boyfriend who promised me the world and then ghosted me... can't even remember his name. I hadn't realised what a heavy load I was carrying.

I did this over and over again, all day long, day after day, until my mind and soul felt clean and light. It was like I had forgotten a bad memory but couldn't quite picture what that bad event was, as there were no dark emotions attached to it. Any scars felt healed and I felt content. It was the most remarkable fast track therapy, ever.

Then, to my joy, I remembered that I was only half way through my journey and realised that I had another three weeks to fill myself up with wonderful things. That made my inner smile even bigger.

SEVENTEEN

26th July: No roads in, no roads out

PHOTO REFS J4 – M4

With that lightness in body and mind, I was already excited about my morning's adventure.

When I first announced my forthcoming journey on Facebook it prompted a comment from an old music industry friend of mine who I'd met 17 years ago. I had produced a couple of music videos for Delays, the band he was managing in 2002, and we had always had a great laugh and connection but, somehow, had lost touch and hadn't seen or spoken for about ten years.

His message asked if I was going to be anywhere near Mallaig and, if I was up for an adventure within an adventure, then I should head out to Inverie on the Knoydart peninsula, aka Scotland's last great wilderness. The warning of no roads in and no roads out was enough to peak my interest. The only way to access Knoydart was either across land via a two day 17-mile mountainous hike or via a small boat. All I needed to do is work out where Mallaig was!

As luck, or fate, would have it, the ferry I had booked from Armadale, Skye went directly to Mallaig. It was a done deal.

Reading the history of Knoydart put an even firmer pin on my map. This was an example of community at its best. The Knoydart Foundation took ownership of the land in 1999, which was a milestone in community land ownership in Scotland and it strongly supports sustainable and ethical businesses. It houses a community of about 100 people, the most remote pub in the British Isles, a café selling locally made pottery, a handful of restaurants and idyllic places to stay, the Knoydart Brewery and a village convenience store. It also offers three famous munros ready for bagging (Larven, Meall Buidhe and Luinne Bheinn), some pretty hardcore hiking trails and off-road cycle tracks for the very hardy. I accepted my friend's mission and told him that I'd call him from the middle of the wilderness.

Sadly, this wasn't an adventure for Charlie or Kenny so I parked Charlie in Mallaig in a nice secure shady spot on the harbour with curtains closed, windows cracked open and food and water out for Kenny. I was nervous about leaving him for a few hours but I just wasn't able to take him with me. I guessed he'd just eat and then find his way under the passenger seat for his daily nap.

I boarded the small boat called Larven, named after one of the munros. It was the most perfect day to cross Loch Nevis. The water was still yet sparkled under the morning sun. Nevis means Heaven and I could see why. Before we set off I watched community spirit at its best as a well-oiled chain gang loaded the boat with bags and boxes of provisions for the people who lived and worked in Knoydart. We pulled in at the pier 30 minutes later, windswept and tasting of salt from the spray, where the second choreographed chain gang unloaded everything on to the pier and the produce was dispersed amongst the residents.

I only had a few hours to wander around before the return boat took me back to Kenny so, like a moth to a flame, I found the Knoydart Brewery. I had a cup of tea on the veranda of the café overlooking the loch and had a rummage around the local shop and bought some locally produced venison chorizo and beers.

I bumped into a couple from the boat who generously invited me to join them for lunch in the pub. This couple's dynamic was that he was the talker and she was the listener. He was tall, lithe and very English and she was small, slightly nervous and Romanian. They'd met online in their 50s and she seemed totally at ease as he told her what order to eat her food in, and when he needed another drink from the bar. Each to their own I guess but they fitted together just right and were comfortable in each other's company. We dined out on fresh seafood, craft ale and shared new stories of life and travels.

As you can imagine there was no 'phone signal on the peninsula so I was unable to call my friend to tell him that Operation Knoydart was a success and had filled my afternoon with joy. I dropped him a WhatsApp message instead in the hope that it would send when I traversed through a Wi-Fi zone in the not too distant future.

I took the opportunity to sit alone on the return boat so I could contemplate. As I sat at the back, I started to feel an emotion that felt like sadness. But it wasn't sadness. I couldn't quite put my finger on it. Now there's nothing like moving across a heavenly loch at speed, with the wind in your hair and spray on your face staring out at beautiful land masses either side to help you figure something out.

It almost felt like that sense of nostalgia when you can feel your heart ache inside your chest. A yearning feeling. I realised that during my time on the road I had met so many grounded people and most of them, if not all, were couples traveling together in their vans. Back home I tend to find spending time with some couples a bit trying as I either feel like the odd one out, or they can bicker and bite at one another regardless of the company around them. I have one couple back home who I always have to say to: *"OK, so no fighting whilst you're out with me please, just be nice!"* They reluctantly agree whilst I sit and wonder what even keeps them together.

But the couples I was meeting over here were the perfect example of two people in harmony with each other. They shared a tiny space and also shared the same values, outlook, humour, hopes, dreams and openly supported and loved each other. I could see how proud they were of each other. I now call it 'The Sticklebrick Effect' where two people find harmony.

I realised that it was this that had set me off. Maybe after my first three weeks of clearing out the crap from my heart and soul, the gap needed to be filled with something more specific.

My relationship history isn't much to write home about. My first four relationships that happened between the ages of 17 and 30 were my most significant. My first boyfriend was my first love and we are still great friends today. I married the second one and, after that ended, I lived with the other two, though obviously not at the same time. All four men were really good men but, for whatever reason I had at the time, it was me that moved on. I was clearly not ready to settle.

I can honestly say that all my other relationships over the past 20 years have been insignificant. In fact, I was pretty delighted when most of them ended as I seemed to have got into a habit of letting the wrong men in. Men who weren't honest, who were pretending to be something they weren't as they didn't like the person they had become. Men living a lie. But, like an onion, it doesn't take long to peel off a few layers revealing a husk of a man inside whilst simultaneously creating a whole load of tears for all involved.

And like most single women, I endured the same old horror stories from the online dating world until I finally grew tired of swiping left and deleted the apps. My online profile tended to attract a menagerie of undersexed, overweight, cross-eyed men in the prime of their midlife crisis. Either that or blokes who thought that never replying or standing someone up on a Friday night was acceptable behaviour. But when my last online encounter threatened to follow me home as he now knew my surname and had found my address, I vowed to find contentment on my own.

But then, whilst sitting on the boat something had clicked and made me feel that maybe the time had come for me to share my life with someone again. Maybe I *was* ready to meet someone. But this time I knew that I'd find them offline.

A decade earlier I had tried to take matters in my own hands and, similar to me trying to Change the Face of the British Film Industry, I set out to Change The Way In Which People Make Friends.

EIGHTEEN

Six dinners later...

Life after Silver Films left me reflecting on life. Not only from a professional perspective but, as a single woman in her 40s, I was still struggling with life alone. Shooting around the world had been so much fun but at the end of the day after a long shoot, when the rest of the crew went back to their rooms to call their husbands, wives and partners, why was I always left chatting to my Dad? No offence Dad.

Where was my partner to call? Where was my soulmate? Why did my friends and I not call each other anymore? My coupled friends were no longer around for chats on the phone and my married ones with kids had dropped off the face of the earth. I guess that was why no one ever really called me. My attempts to arrange nights out with friends were also proving frustrating as their busy lifestyles only offered windows in their diaries three months in advance.

Was it too late to make new friends? But where do you find this rare breed?

One of the biggest things I was missing was decent conversation. Online dating rendered superficial chats, especially when you walked into the rendezvous and knew instantly that you wanted to leave. Whereas chatting at dinner parties with friends was always great fun and I loved going to them... hang on a minute, when was the last time I was invited to a dinner party? The 'single' dinner guest is an awkward guest to invite so you end up being unconsciously struck off the list.

But that generated a spark in my head, which built to a flame. A flame I just couldn't put out.

What if *I* could create something, an opportunity, a platform for the forgotten guests of the world to get offline and meet face to face with like-minded people? What if they could be brought together over a dinner party scenario in someone's home? What if some old-fashioned values were chucked into the mix like trust, honesty and reliability? What if... *I* could actually create this?

And it all kicked off from there. Another unexpected turn on the path with a neon flashing signpost - wonky road ahead.

The redecoration of my sitting room began. Not with a fresh lick of a delicious sounding paint like Eating Room Red from Farrow & Ball, but with multicoloured Post It notes filling the walls with ideas and thoughts that wouldn't stop flowing.

I then leapt into an unknown digital abyss of logic and coding to create a website. Talk about living outside one's comfort zone! I hate technology! But I love logic and the Post It notes soon changed shape as the logic developed around the room and coloured threads started to join them together.

This led to the birth and launch of Six Dinners Later... The name and the ellipsis said it all. After six dinners anything could happen.

Here's how it worked. A cycle began by a someone joining the guest list and getting invited to their first dinner party by a host they didn't know. They had to dig deep to attend that first dinner with five 'strangers' but their courage was rewarded. After that first dinner it was then their turn to reciprocate and arrange their own dinner by inviting their original host and four new people off the list. After hosting their dinner it was then time to sit back and enjoy being invited to a dinner party by each of their guests. Over a round of six dinners you got to meet twenty-five new people.

What was interesting, and completely fortuitous, was that if you looked at all the connections that would be made from a whole round six dinners it made a community of 150. In the 1990s a famous anthropologist discovered that the optimum size for a perfect community to thrive and maintain stable social relationships is... 150, aka Dunbar's Number. The stars were aligning.

The first dinner was hosted on the 6th June 2012, which also coincided with the Transit of Venus. It felt right to ride on the back of an astronomical phenomenon.

And it worked. Venus's transit between the Sun and Earth was recorded and over the next two years brave and interesting people were signing up, being invited, attending dinners, hosting their own, having great conversations and making new friends. It wasn't a supper club as the focus wasn't on the food. It was about the power of breaking bread together.

And the dinners ranged from fancy three coursers by hosts with a flair for flavours to one party host who had no clue in the kitchen and only had five chairs in her flat. She got everyone to make their own crêpes on rotation in her tiny kitchen with the person without a chair being the one at the stove and round they went. The feedback from that dinner party was epic.

I also enjoyed hosting several dinners myself including takeaway fish'n'chips eaten off a newspaper tablecloth, an Easter lunch for waifs and strays who found themselves alone during the Bank Holiday and a dinner for twelve on Valentine's day called Screw Love, hosted at my house. The joy was that I also got to meet so many amazing people, shared some hilarious evenings and conversations and grew my friendship group faster than I could have imagined. Because this wasn't a dating site my friends joined in too and hosted their own dinners, some of which I would attend so it ironically became a very long way round to getting to see my original friends!

By this time, I had attracted an investor and together we worked tirelessly developing and upgrading the site, marketing, maintaining the guests and their requests. But we were growing faster than the money was coming in and we soon realised that this idea was bigger than the both of us. We needed to raise significant investment in order to keep the momentum going. But we needed money soon.

The only way to raise quick cash was to sell assets. So I started selling mine. My car and motorbike were first to go (both with tears in my eyes) then clothes and shoes, but when I got close to putting my flat on the market, my Dad, who never interfered with my businesses, vehemently insisted I thought again. But the only way to survive this would be to sell my flat and live off the proceeds in the hope that we could make it work in time.

He reminded me that I had cleverly and successfully navigated my way out of Silver Films without too much financial loss but the potential loss and sacrifice from trying to keeping Six Dinners Later... alive would be greater.

Dad wasn't a risk taker so how would he know how close I was getting to making this work? This idea was becoming tangible. People were making new friendships. How could I walk away from something that was working (albeit at the risk of my health and wealth). It was actually bringing people together in the way I had intended so how could I let them down? And how could I let my friends down who all believed in what I was doing and would say, "*If anyone can make this work it's YOU!*"

At the eleventh hour I decided not to sell my flat but, the truth of the matter was, I'd totally run out of funds and it was starting to seriously affect my personal life and wellbeing. I was no longer able to eat properly, let alone host a dinner party and be part of this community that I had created. This irony wasn't lost on me. My Mother Hubbard cupboards were literally bare and I'd wake up hungry and go to sleep hungry. The moment I walked past one of the bagel shops on Brick Lane and managed to scrape together 25p to buy a plain bagel was the day I knew this had to stop.

It took me back to my Silver Films days when I was holding on by my fingernails to a dream that I couldn't touch. Why did I keep making such difficult life choices? Why couldn't I be satisfied with a nine to five Monday to Friday job? Why did I keep falling at the last hurdle? It was exhausting, confusing and heartbreaking. It's like bringing children in to the world and then having to give them away.

As hard as I had tried, I just couldn't find a way forward so, with gritted teeth and the heaviest heart, I closed my Six Dinners Later... chapter and walked away.

Even though it was comforting to know that guests and hosts who met through the dinners were still in touch with each other, I underestimated the level of grief I was about to deal with when I let it go. I'm totally aware that no one actually died here but it was tough to move on from something I had created, loved and nurtured and had been in my waking and sleeping thoughts for so long. There are no books called How To Grieve When Your Company Goes Down, no groups for entrepreneurs to join, no one to really talk to.

Once the website had been taken down there was no physical record of it. As if it had never happened. It left like a strange dream that had left me in limbo and in debt. I wasn't able to share the pain with anyone as I knew they were not able to fully empathise. So, as ever, the only option was to just get on with it. I think my friends assumed I was fine but, my goodness, I wasn't. The barriers just went up and the skin thickened.

Now what? Breathe. What do I do next? Pace. How do I earn money? Panic. I'm unemployable! Sigh.

•

A couple of months of pacing and panic followed with no clear solution. Then my friend, the one I met at Granada Studios Tour, spotted a job on an industry Facebook page looking for someone to cover maternity for the head of an advertising awards ceremony called the British Arrows. I'd never heard of them but they needed someone who understood the advertising industry, who could run a company, had experience of producing live events and was able to start immediately. Oh, I guess that's me!

One meeting later, I was offered the job and started the next day.

Blimey, I wasn't expecting that! They paid me a ridiculously low fee but I let them as I was just delighted, and totally relieved, to be actually earning anything. I could buy food again. I could meet my friends again. I felt alive again. One thing I'd never anticipated was for the CEO to never return after her maternity and that I would then stay for six years and end up as Managing Director and a member of one of the most prestigious boards in advertising.

But by my fourth year I knew this was not my vocation. It had been a fun ride and I'd met some fabulous people along the way, but being given the sole task of arranging a huge event for over a thousand industry people to get drunk on one night felt a tad vacuous. It filled my bank but it certainly didn't fill my soul. And my soul needed attention. We were also totally understaffed and by the end of each event I pretty much collapsed with the stress. I felt that if all this energy, effort and talent were placed elsewhere, perhaps within the charitable sector, I knew that I could make a difference, rather than just putting on a glorified piss-up. So I resigned.

My resignation wasn't accepted and it was then that I was promoted to MD, placed on the board with a healthy pay rise. But for me that wasn't what it was about. Status and money had never been a driver in my decision making so the Chairman asked me what would it take to make me stay. I thought long and hard and finally suggested that, as the company was so well connected and respected, we should use that to an advantage. The advertising industry was predominately white, middle class male and I mooted the idea that we were in the perfect position to change that. We could put an end to nepotism by being the conduit for young people of colour, or from disadvantaged backgrounds, to find paid jobs in the creative industry.

So that's what I did. I stayed and, with the backing of the board, I set up BAD (British Arrows Doorway) an initiative that successfully found paid jobs for young people who would have never have had the opportunity to work in the advertising industry. And it worked. It bloody worked!

It was so fulfilling to create and deliver something that had a tangible effect. Not just on the young people securing their dream jobs, but in changing the opinions of their parents and family who hadn't believed the creative industry was an option for their children and had positively discouraged it.

In the lead up to the 2019 show I knew it was going to be my last. I had taken the awards ceremony as far as I could and I knew that BAD could run itself so, in true form, I moved on.

NINETEEN

27th July: I know where I am going

I landed back in Mallaig feeling totally refreshed and clear headed. Mallaig itself was a sweet little port town with a few shops and bars but, apart from buying a Harris tweed cushion to match Charlie's interior, I didn't linger too long as I needed to get to the Isle of Mull in the next couple of days.

I had a couple of friends – and these two are perfect for each other – who spend a week at Fidden Farm in Fionphort on the south westerly tip of Mull every year and the timing was just right to meet up with them. I'd heard wondrous things about the hidden white beaches and I was ready for some sand between my toes.

I drove to Kilchoan to catch my fifth boat. I was already feeling like an old seadog when it came to boarding as I knew which lane to approach in, when to drive on, how close to park to the van in front, where the plugs to recharge tech on the boats were, and my Wi-Fi clicked on automatically. I also knew that, if I was lucky, I could be out on deck being flanked by dolphins and minke whales leaping through the waves. It's one hell of a commute!

The ferry brought me in to the colourful port town of Tobermory positioned on a steep hill with terraces of houses and gardens looking out to sea. Multi-coloured shops, bars and restaurants lined the main road facing the sea and, if it hadn't been raining when I arrived, I could have been on the Riviera.

I had only planned to stay for one night but wasn't prepared to pitch up in the main carpark with the other unimaginative motorhome owners. Instead, I found the nearest campsite to the port about three miles up the hill and settled down for an early night. Kenny, who had missed me during my Knoydart adventure, was wide awake and began his nightly ritual of scampering, jumping, playing and pacing. It wasn't the best night's sleep I'd had but it was lovely to be back in the van with my favourite companion.

That night I heard back from my music industry friend, who had recommended Knoydart in the first place. He was delighted that I'd completed my mission and told me that I was now the only other person he knew who had ever been there. I remembered that he lived opposite Hilbre Island, off the Wirral coast, and he sent me photos of his stunning sunsets. We both agreed that it had been way too long since our last get together so I suggested that I could 'swing by' on my way back to London. This also meant that I could add another island and one final beautiful vista on to my trip before the greyness, coldness and claustrophobia of London took hold once again.

•

I awoke early to find Kenny snoring away, exhausted by his extreme nocturnal activities. He pretty much sleeps 75% of the day so there wouldn't be much movement from him for the rest of the day.

I tidied the van, cooked some breakfast, had a lovely hot shower and then sat and pondered for a while about the day ahead whilst a light rain fell. No specific plan came to mind and I wasn't in a hurry so I indulged in some 'empty head' time. I enjoy these moments and can do it at home for hours as there are no external distractions from children or partners. It's almost like meditation but without the formalities of chanting or breathing. It's literally doing nothing and I can feel my thoughts fall into place like feathers falling to the ground in slow motion.

A friend recently asked me what I did when I did nothing. I found it rather an odd question and couldn't work out why she needed to ask anyone how to do it. But it seems there is an art to doing nothing whilst gaining a sense of fulfilment. And the big secret is... it's OK to do nothing! It's OK to look and not think. No coulda shoulda woulda's filling your thoughts. No monkey chatter. No guilt. Just enjoy the moment and breathe.

I guess that's what mindfulness is all about, but the whole 'mindfulness' conversation bores me. Just get on with it. I'm not a yoga person either but I do like a good old stretch and a bit of deep breathing in the morning or evening and, to be honest, a few minutes of that each day is enough for me.

The rain had stopped so I wandered down the hill into the town. It felt like a metropolis compared to what I was used to. I had repeatedly driven through one-horse towns, most without a horse, and had learnt to fuel myself and the van wherever the opportunity arose. But Tobermory was very different; I felt the need to see what it had to offer.

I started at the aquarium on the west side of the port. It hosted locally caught sea creatures that resided there for around four weeks to then be returned to the ocean. Like an aquatic city break for nature. They had a touch pool so the kids could get an upfront and personal view and get their hands on a twelve-legged starfish or be squirted at by a cheeky scallop.

Next stop, and literally next door, was the Tobermory distillery. The tours weren't running that day so I went straight to the shop. I've now realised that when you have time on your hands, and no agenda, you are able to hold longer, more in-depth conversations with people and actually listen to their stories. I seem to have hurried my way through life not learning enough about other people so now I was enjoying meeting people again.

I would put money on it that I was the only one who had visited the distillery that morning who was given a private rendition in their private bar of a song called *Horizons*, written and performed by one of the guys that worked there. He had moved there in his 60s and taken up the guitar and acting. He told me about the open mic session he was hosting that night up the hill near the big hotel. I hoped they might have a tambourine to hand as that is my only instrument of ability. I bought a bottle of the 12-year Tobermory and it will always remind of that song.

I had lunch at Café Fish, recommended by guitar man, and had quite possibly the most delicious halibut I've ever had. A huge steak of white fish with flavours of freshness that only come from a fish caught a few meters away. As I paid the bill I saw three women take their seats. With a smile I recommended my fish dish to them. "*Is it fried?*" one asked with a grating American accent and a grimace. Whatever.

I walked past the local church hall to see a notice for a screening of *I Know Where I'm Going*, the classic Powell Pressburger film from the 40s. I absolutely love their films with *A Matter of Life and Death* being in my top ten. But this earlier film had actually been shot in Tobermory and had been recommended to me by a new friend who I had recently met on cycling tour of the Alps.

I should be clear that I wasn't *riding* the alps, I was *driving* the camera support vehicle for the Fireflies Cycling Club. The club was set up to raise money for leukaemia and blood cancers by riding 750 miles from Austria to Cannes in eight days. Their motto is 'For Those Who Suffer We Ride'. And they certainly did suffer. It's a truly gruelling ride. As a new cyclist I wasn't fit enough to do the ride so I volunteered to drive the camera car with the photographer. Those cyclists were my heroes and heroines as I watched them fight the elements and their own personal traumatic stories of cancer to get to the end and raise much needed funds.

So, it was one of these riders who told me about the film and I was meant to watch it before I set off. But now, here it was in Tobermory in the village hall. The problem was it was showing four days later. I was so tempted to sit it out to see the film but I knew I couldn't sit still for that long. I decided to make it the first film I watched on my return to reality. And it was. (It's not as good as *A Matter of Life and Death*!)

I wandered back to the van to read a bit more of my third book. Yes, third book! I'd started Nan Shepherd's *The Living Mountain*. She writes beautifully and poetically about the Cairngorm Plateau but for me it's still quite a hard read. Luckily, they're short stories that work well with my attention span. My lunchtime wine was making me sleepy so I settled down for a rare daytime disco nap with Kenny. I awoke a couple of hours later, still sleepy.

Yawning and stretching, I could have taken the easy route and just stayed in but I thought no, I'll go out as I'd promised to go to the open mic night. As a solo traveller, and indeed a single person, this is when you have to dig deep and force yourself out as you have no one with you spurring you on saying *"Come on lazy pants, it's going to be fun!"* You just gotta do it yourself.

At 7.30pm I walked a different route to the town past the Western Isles Hotel and instantly recognised the famous revolving doors from *I Know Where I'm Going.* I still get a kick out of seeing film locations. I turned the corner to see the venue of where I was going... It was an ugly new hotel. My heart sank a bit. Come on... keep going.

I walked into an empty, brightly lit bar that looked like an old man's drinking saloon and felt a little lost. Keep going... Seeing my lost face, an old guy propping up the bar jokingly asked if I was one of the acts.

"If only I'd brought my tambourine..." I replied. He laughed and turned out to be a regular fixture at the bar, founder of the local Veterans Brewery and the owner of Brown's, the only licenced ironmongers in the country. Established in 1830, he sells an eclectic mix of items from two-inch bolts and whisky to mini fried egg pans and banjoleles. He bought me a bottle of 303, his own brewed beer. This was a good enough start to get me settled.

It was open mic night so anything could happen. A sturdy woman in her 60s wearing a floral dress with a pink ribbon was singing Irish rebel songs accompanied by her guitar. My veteran ironmonger was not impressed and heckled from the back. I found out she was from San

Diego and competing in three Highland games over the next week and was one of the strongest contenders in Tossing the Caber. The weight of a caber does not change for women and I realised that her sturdiness was pure muscle. I could hear *The Twilight Zone* theme tune playing in my head.

By my third bottle of 303, I seemed to be fully ensconced with the locals. I'd met the dentist, who'd moved to Tobermory three months ago from Edinburgh. She had been pretty high up in the dental reconstruction world but wanted to step back from the perfectly whitened and straightened teeth of the city and randomly applied for a job in Tobermory. She was more surprised when she got the job and now lived in house overlooking the harbour. I also met the local gardener, a gentle handsome 45-year-old man rooted by nature who lived like a Romany in a shepherd's hut.

When you've been on the road for a while it's really comforting to find yourself in the middle of drunken tittle-tattle and local gossip, hearing about faceless names who said this and did that. *"Oh she didn't did she?"* Apparently, she did! They took me on a late night tour of the town, we had a wee dram or two in their local pub and all ended up in the dentist's house for more whisky. Drunk! I got home at 1.30am. That was a most unexpected and fun day!

I loved Tobermory and could have stayed there till the film screening, but this littlest hobo knew she had to get going the next morning.

TWENTY

29th July: Familiar faces and hidden beaches

PHOTO REFS J3 – K3

It was a much longer drive than I had anticipated to get to the next campsite but I didn't mind. The coastal roads through the Isle of Mull running alongside the Atlantic Ocean were particularly stunning. The road had been carved into the edge of the mountain with the outer edge of the road dropping directly down to the sea. Charlie hugged the corners with confidence whilst I indulged in the odd look out of my open window to the horizon when the road straightened.

For several miles, a road cyclist was my only companion as I drove and he rode at the same speed. He'd overtake me then I'd overtake him and so it went on for miles and miles with smiles and waves each time. He was my road buddie.

Along the way, I drove past a field full of black sheep with just one white one. *"Curiouser and curiouser,"* I mused as I tried to decipher its meaning. Was the white sheep now the black sheep? Or had the outcasts become the norm? Could this be a repeat of *Animal Farm* but with sheep? I would have loved to have had a deep and meaningful conversation with someone about this but my cycling buddie had taken a different path so he was not an option. Kenny offered no insight. He wasn't the greatest debating buddie in a van. The concept consumed my thoughts for quite a while, and still does.

In fact, after a 90-minute phone call with my poet sister, nine months later, we worked it out. The striking image of the black flock with the single white sheep within was Yin. The feminine side of Tao. Maybe this road trip had invited balance into my life and, after all my years of feeling either asexual or a tad masculine, was this a sign that a new feminine butterfly was emerging. Flutter flutter?

After a five-hour drive I finally arrived at Fidden Farm and was greeted by the familiar smiles and laughter of my friend and his lovely wife. We used to hang out during our Haçienda days in Manchester and had met during the initial rise of The Stone Roses. In fact we saw them in Paris, Amsterdam and the infamous Spike Island gig. Best daze ever!

The next couple of days felt like being on holiday with old chums, which I was! They took me on a long walk across marshes and craggy rocks to find the hidden beaches. The first one could have been a poster campaign for Thailand's tourist board, but we didn't stop there. Oh no, we continued walking to reveal the next beach. Was I in the Maldives? Can we stay here please? No, let's keep walking as it just gets better. And it did. The only difference between the Maldives and Mull was that we were the only people on the beach with no one selling holiday tat. Shallow blue waters stretching out across clear pale sand to tiny rocky islands disappearing off into the distance. The silent flight of the puffins adhering to the call for quiet. It actually takes a while to compute as you think that the VW camper has doubled as a teleportation pod and dropped you on the edge of paradise.

It was a wonderful pause in my whole crazy journey.

On my last night I was lying in my van trying to sleep but kept hearing strange noises. I couldn't work it out. I knew it wasn't sheep surrounding the van but it was an unfamiliar sound. I woke at around 4am and looked out the back window. I tended not to draw the curtains at the back as my bike rack and bike covered most of the window. But as I looked out I saw the familiar shape of Kenny climbing up the bike rack.

"*Ah, sweet,*" I thought and turned over to get more sleep. And then sat bolt upright! "*What the hell is Kenny doing outside at four in the morning?!!*"

I leapt out of bed, threw on some clothes and jumped out of the van. Kenny was happily padding about on the roof and I could see from the amount of paw prints that he had been roaming around for quite some time. Well that was the mystery noise solved. But how the hell did he get out? He had little cold wet paws from the morning dew and he calmly trotted over when he saw me. I had no idea how long he had been out but I gave him an early morning bowl of food which he inhaled. I still have no clue as to how he got out but am astonished that he knew where home was especially when his home kept moving. He is a remarkable cat.

It had been a glorious couple of days so when I announced that I was leaving in the morning my friend couldn't understand why I would want to leave such a magical place so soon. I couldn't quite explain that this wasn't a holiday for me. This wasn't about chilling out with friends and having a fabulous time. Lovely as that was, this was about throwing caution to the wind, leaping out of the comfort zone and embarking on a life journey. And although I was sad to be leaving them, I had to leave.

TWENTY-ONE

31st July: Jeremiah 29:11-13

I estimated the drive to the ferry port in Craignure to be about two hours but I left plenty of time just in case. The ferry would take me to Oban, the home of another great whisky, whose distillery I was looking forward to visiting. It was a very handsome town with tiers of old, historic buildings climbing up the hill. I was surprised to see an incongruous looking Coliseum right at the top. I knew I would be investigating that later.

Upon learning that Oban, the whisky, was now owned by Diageo, the corporate giant, it immediately lost its appeal. I'm a lover and supporter of the independent world so a multi-brand held no interest, even in dram form. The first thing I did after finding my campsite was to find a good whisky shop. As many shops did, there was a wee space set aside for tasting and that morning they were offering ones I had never encountered before.

GlenDronach is a 12-year-old malt matured in a combination of Spanish Pedro Ximenez and Oloroso sherry casks which gives it a beautifully smooth sweet experience. It has now become my favourite whisky ever.

With a cup of tea and cake from a little café, I climbed the steep climb to the Coliseum and settled in the centre, in the sunshine, and finished my book. It was a spectacular view of the bay and, as I circled the internal circumference, the stone arches created perfect triptychs of the sea dotted with fishing boats.

As a big round red sun sank into the sea I tallied up my fifth fish'n'chips of the trip. I sat on a wall on the pier until the final blue flash brought daylight to an official end.

•

So far during my journey, Charlie had been incredibly well behaved and I thanked him every day for being such a good boy and not leaving me stranded in the middle of nowhere. Apart from his screaming brakes that made me hold my breath, whilst my knuckles whitened as I gripped the steering wheel on steep descents, the only thing that had been playing up was the fridge. Since his re-wiring in Applecross he had been much better, but this morning, no matter how much fiddling and flicking of the wires I could do, I couldn't get any current flowing. I feared the battery had died a death.

The leisure battery was a necessity as it powered the fridge, my mobile, iPad and Kenny's twin fan air-cooling system and, as chilled wines and beers for the evenings were a must, I finally succumbed to the fact that we needed to visit a garage.

I asked the chap at the campsite if he knew anything about batteries but alas he didn't. He pointed me in the direction of Trail West Garage in town.

"*He mends old Land Rovers and trailers. He'll be the man to see,*" he told me, though I couldn't quite see the connection. I called him anyway and explained the problem. He sounded busy, however he reluctantly agreed that I could bring Charlie to him that morning.

Good old Charlie. He always brings the best out in people so, in no time, this monosyllabic gnarled Scottish mechanic was smiling and sharing personal stories about his youth, his relationship with VWs, his dream of living in a van and embarking on his own road trip – if only his wife would let him. We had such a laugh together. He made me cups of tea and brought me oatie biscuits and I helped him hold wires in place as he soldered the fresh wires of a new, and more powerful, leisure battery in place. I could have stayed all day. It was such a sweet three hours.

When Charlie was ready to go, I went through to his office to pay the bill. As soon as I walked in I stopped dead. I'd never seen a messier office.

Papers and boxes (his filing system) covered in oil and precariously piled high and balanced on flimsy tables taking the strain. Blackened engine parts covered the floor with the darkest of kitchens in the far corner. I then realised where that hint of oil in my tea and on my oaties had come from. I was tempted to offer to tidy it for him! He must have seen my face and said his daughter was always on his back to tidy up but he convinced me that he knew where everything was. Organised chaos or denial. Either way it suited him down to the ground.

As he handed my bank card back to me he took my hand and held my gaze. He told me that it had been an honour to meet me. Then, in true Scottish Christian style, he quoted *"For I know the plans I have for you"* declared the Lord, *"plans to prosper you and not to harm you, plans to give you hope and future."* Jeremiah 29:11-13.

To be honest, anything religious like that makes me feel rather awkward, possibly a throwback to my convent school days, but it suited the situation. Not quite knowing what to reply, I just smiled and thanked him for a lovely day.

I left the garage with an affirmation that my instincts and decisions were all moving in the right direction and that my actions and demeanour were of the person I wanted to be. I was also relieved to hear that God knew my plans as I certainly didn't but, with or without God, I felt something was falling into place.

Kenny was happy that his air-cooled system was managing his temperature once again and he settled down with his whiskers blowing in the wind. I drove away happy that my wines and beers were nicely chilling and wondering what the next turn of the road would bring.

TWENTY-TWO

3rd Aug: Are you sponsored by Bruichladdich?

PHOTO REFS L3 – Q5

Some paths are so unexpected I couldn't make them up.

I had now completed all my pre-booked hopscotch ferries but I knew I wasn't ready to head home just yet. To keep me on the road, and sea, for a little longer I decided to add a trilogy of Isles to my journey, so ferries to Islay, Jura and Arran were purchased at Oban port.

It was 10am by the time I left my campsite and tootled south out of Oban. My ferry to Islay wasn't until that evening so I had, what I thought, was a great idea.

My cunning plan was to catch the 6pm ferry to Islay that took two hours and then jump on the 8.30pm council ferry to Jura. I was going to wild camp near the port and then, in the morning, drive as far north as the road would take me (there is in fact only one road on Jura). I'd park Charlie up, give Kenny breakfast and a quick tickle under the chin and then walk the last four miles north along a dirt track to find the house that George Orwell lived in to write *1984*. He wrote it in 1948 and some believe he just inverted the date to come up with the title. I hope that's true.

I reckoned that this would be a great day. Though by 8pm that evening I'd learnt to not bother making plans again...

I had a whole day to fill before my ferry so I decided to follow a random road off the atlas that led to nowhere. I stopped briefly as I couldn't resist the urge not to play Talking Heads' *Road To Nowhere*. After a few zig zags and a 15% climb that, for Charlie, required a similar effort as did I on the bike, I was rewarded by a perfectly symmetrical stone hump-backed bridge over a wide glimmering river. The bridge had two circles either side of the arch anthropomorphising him into a cute little character with big eyes and a gaping mouth. I parked up and sat on a stone step on the banks. To my right there was a wee gallery with unusual paintings and photography that operated an honesty box system.

Honesty boxes are a big thing in the remote areas of Scotland and it's a real treat when you find one. I'd be driving down a road in the middle of nowhere and find a pile of egg boxes at the side of the road, decorated with flowers, filled with fresh eggs from the local farm and a little money box next to it. One place I found was a deserted farm shop with a huge array of meats and cheeses and beers and wines in chilled cabinets. The self-service till was a book to write down what you'd taken and a chip and pin device to pay through. Fabulous!

Nothing took my fancy at the gallery so I drove down towards the 'no through road' into the village of Easdale, only to realise I was lucky enough to make it in time for the finale of their Scarecrow Festival 2019! This wasn't any old village, this was, well I don't quite know what?! As I drove along the approach road I witnessed a road traffic accident, a surgeon operating on a patient, a deep sea diver hanging in mid-air, the ugliest mermaid and a drunk woman in a pink tutu smoking a fag! Thankfully, all were scarecrows but the now familiar *Twilight Zone* theme tune was playing loudly on repeat.

I got to the tiny village centre where symmetrical rows of single-story white terraces were home to the locals. In the centre, a band of old timers were playing their fiddles, accordions and drums entertaining a tiny crowd. Every house in the village had also put weeks of creativity and effort (possibly drug induced) into their entry and each manifestation sat boss-eyed with a thousand mile stare. I don't know about the crows but some certainly scared the b'jesus out of me.

The Oyster Bar was open serving tea and bacon sandwiches so I sat on the terrace overlooking some small islands with my cuppa and bacon sarnie. I heard the distorted voice of a man through a tannoy in the square announcing that there was one seat left on the rib boat taking people around Easdale Island so I jumped up and paid my £5 for the last seat on the boat. With life jacket strapped on we zoomed around the island for a five-minute water-based tour! By noon I was back in Charlie heading south to the port.

•

It was a two-hour ferry ride to Islay and I arrived right on time with 30 minutes to find my next ferry. I drove down the ramp from the boat and, while still sitting in Charlie, I leant out of the window to ask the first person I saw where I get the ferry to Jura.

Before I even opened my mouth he asked *"Are you here for the bike ride tomorrow?"*

"Eh?" I replied eloquently.

"Are you sponsored by Bruichladdich?" Bruichladdich is one of eight distilleries on this tiny isle.

"I have no idea what you're talking about!!" I said, suddenly sounding rather too English.

"Well there's a 100-mile ride around the island tomorrow and, as your campervan and bike handlebars are the exact same colour as the distillery colours, I just thought that's why you were here. I thought they'd sent you!"

"Oh!" I laughed, *"No! I was just going to go ask you where I get the ferry to Jura! But funnily enough I was meant to be doing the 100-mile ride in London tomorrow for UNICEF and already have sponsors in place so... why not, I'm in! I can always go to Jura tomorrow."*

"Great!" he said with a beaming smile. *"Follow me and I'll show you a campsite where some of the other riders are staying. And anyway, Jura's covered in midges this year and they have no internet so you're better off with us!"*

And with that, my best laid plans changed and off we went. It turned out that not only was he the organiser of the 100-mile ride but he also ran the Post Office, the SPAR in Port Charlotte, and the petrol station which only had one pump named Pumpy McPumpface. He was definitely the man to know.

Before we set off he picked up a guy who had bizarrely just arrived from the Gold Coast and was waiting at a bus stop with a small suitcase. There were no buses so he was bundled into his car and offered to take him to his hotel.

However, on the way to his hotel, and my campsite, something snapped under my right foot and I realised that my accelerator had broken. It just flapped below my foot like a loose tooth and Charlie started to grind to a halt.

I flashed my lights hoping that he'd seen my distress signal but all I could see was his red back lights disappearing in to the distance. Yep, the inevitable had just happened. It was breakdown time. I sat and wondered what to do. But then, like an edit in a film with hero music cued perfectly, I saw his white headlights reappearing over the hill and he came back to find me.

"*Do you know anything about vans?*" I asked them both.

"*Nope!*" they answered in unison.

The hero music scratched to a halt. I then remembered my mechanics' last words to me, "...*call me anywhere, anytime...*" and, with a hesitant smile and crossed fingers, I called him at 8.45pm on a Saturday night. He was in! Cue hero music again as he talked us through how to do a quick fix so I could get to the campsite.

"*Right Janey, go to the engine, there's a spring on the left hand side. Pull it back and then secure it in position with one of the cable ties I gave you, but not too far. This will give you enough revs to ride the clutch to get to the campsite.*"

"*Amazing! Thank you!!*" I had no idea what he was talking about! But between the three of us we managed to work it out. One cable tie later and one throttle spring in position I managed to *ride the clutch* for eight miles at 10mph to the campsite. It was very exciting and I giggled all the way!

I parked up at the campsite said good night to my local hero and prepared some power food ahead of my mega ride. I was in bed by 11pm too tired to notice the wind and rain building around me.

·

I woke nervously with a "*WTF?!*" at the front of my mind and flutters in my stomach. "*What the hell have I got myself into now...?!*" With an unknown day ahead of me, with a bunch of strangers and a broken-down van, this was going to be a challenge. It was 8.45am. Power breakfast eaten, power shower taken and I was ready to go. The fog was low, the rain was hard and the wind was strong.

About 50 riders gathered at the local café where we were handed out maps to be folded and stored somewhere dry and we set off. Within no time I found myself near the back, which is my usual position on every ride. I was accompanied by a chap in his 60s with a jolly face who moved to the isle about 15 years ago. He was a plumber and had married the local police chief's daughter so he was accepted into the village quicker than most. He was the one who had fitted the powerful showers in the campsite so I thanked him for that. We rode at a similar pace and chatted away for hours through rain, gale-force winds, sun, food breaks, loo breaks and lunch at the Ardbeg distillery. A wee dram was much needed to aid the return ride.

The head wind had been unbearably strong on the first leg, so much so that we were almost cycling backwards. He kindly got me to tuck in behind him so he could take the brunt of the force and save my energy. On the return leg, and true to Scottish form, the headwind was right back in our faces so we assumed the previous position. We got to a junction where we had a choice of route and, because of the wind and our achy legs, we decided to take the slightly shorter option. I therefore didn't manage the whole 100 miles, but 76 miles was further than I'd ever ridden, so I was pretty chuffed with that.

I got back to the campsite feeling exceedingly relieved. What a crazy 24 hours! After another hot shower my wobbly legs made it to the pub to meet my cycling buddie and his wife for a few numbing whiskies and finally fell into bed with Kenny, totally exhausted, knowing I'd have to deal with Charlie in the morning.

TWENTY-THREE

5th Aug: Not all breakdowns are bad

PHOTO REFS R5 – R3

Why does the sun tend to shine the day after a long windy rainy ride?! Anyway, I dragged my aching body out of bed on this sunny morning, with a looming feeling of needing to get Charlie back on the road. I had no clue as to how to go about this as, during the ride, I'd found out that the only mechanic on the isle was away for three days at a funeral, so an alternative plan would need to be hatched.

I walked down to the Post Office and was greeted by my original hero and his friend who, was not only on holiday in Islay for a few days but also owned an old Land Rover. On face value, that didn't sound like a solution but, he had time on his hands, he was an engineer and, like all engineers, was up for a challenge so in my eyes he was a great solution! Back on the campsite, I introduced him to Charlie, handed him the spare throttle cable, my How To Keep Your Volkswagen Alive manual and made him a cup of tea. In no time, all I could see were his legs protruding from underneath the van.

He reminded me of a younger version of my Dad, in fact their dress code was almost identical. Dad was always up for a challenge (or a reason to hide away in the garage) and, to the dismay of my Mum, he could mend everything. So she never got her new cooker, car, television, VHS player, etc as Dad would emerge from the garage gleaming with pride, to the silent sighs and fake smiles from Mum, as her 1970s hairdryer, heavy as a brick with just the one speed, lived to blow another day.

It would have been so much easier with Charlie up on some ramps but my new friend seemed rather content crawling around on his back on the grass. In order to get the cable threaded through a pipe to the back, some of the engine parts needed to be removed so we lined them up carefully on the grass in order of removal. More tea was made.

About an hour later, Charlie was the proud owner of a perfectly fitted new throttle cable. And it worked! All three of us were totally amazed and delighted. It was hitting midday so I offered to buy him lunch before I caught the afternoon ferry and we decided to drive to Portnahaven to do some seal watching. We then popped into a little gallery along the way, had another cup of tea and finally said goodbye to each other as I headed off to the port.

My plan (remember not to make plans on a road trip) was to then jump on the afternoon ferry up to Jura to complete Operation 1984.

As I drove off, I caught a flickering warning light out of the corner of my eye. By the time I could see that it was something to do with the electrics, Charlie completely lost power. Another WTF moment! I turned the key a couple more times but nothing. Luckily, we hadn't even got out of the driveway of the gallery so my friend was still driving behind me. He jumped out of his Land Rover.

"It's not the throttle is it? Has it snapped?" He asked nervously in case he'd broken Charlie.

"No, the cable's good! I've just lost all power...?!"

Upon inspection, and a bit of engine fiddling, he concluded that it was the alternator as no power was going to the battery.

"But the alternator's only 13 months old... it can't be that!" I said bemused. So, I called my mechanic.

"But the alternator's only 13 months old... it can't be that!" he said confidently. *"I fitted it!!"*

We jump-started the battery and drove back to the campsite where Charlie assumed his stationary position. My stand-in Dad Jr. reckoned that if the battery could be fully charged overnight, then it would have enough power to get me off the isle in the morning, onto a boat, off the boat and to a garage on the mainland. All I needed to do was find a garage on the mainland that knew about classic VWs. So, we took the battery over to our friend at the Post Office for an overnight charge.

It was late afternoon by now and I knew I wasn't going to get off the isle that day, which meant that Jura and Arran would have to be struck off my list. I was suddenly engulfed by a dark wave of having to return home sooner rather than later so I allowed the faint thought of "*Maybe I could just stay here for a while and not go home...*" flutter in my mind for longer than it should. But with a sigh and a snap back to reality I knew I had to go. Damn.

The silver lining to my predicament came in the form of an invitation to dinner with the whole Post Office / SPAR / petrol station family. Venison casserole, a selection of Islay Ales and several drams later down the pub. The kindness and generosity of people filled my heart. A lovely homely night for a little lost traveller who wandered back to her immobile camper a wee bit drunk, but smiling.

My morning schedule felt like being back at work as there were several moving parts that needed to be whipped into shape, in the right order, for me to successfully get off the island by noon. There was only one ferry that day so the countdown clock had begun. I set up my makeshift office in the campsite café, pulled my producer hat well and truly on, and went off at high speed. It had been a while since I'd used this part of my brain so I hoped that it still worked.

My first phone call revealed that getting a breakdown vehicle to pick me up on the isle wasn't really going to be an option as it would take far too long. So, after a long chat with my breakdown company they suggested that, if my battery allowed, I should try to get Charlie off the isle, on to the mainland and drive as far as I could. They would then pick me up from wherever I'd got to. Fair enough.

I then needed to find a specialist VW garage. After many phone calls, the only one that could fit me in, was in Stirling, 130 miles away from my mainland drop off! But I had no choice. VWs can't go to any old garage, so Stirling it was.

If the alternator was to blame then I needed to get a new one sent to the garage in Stirling in time. I called my VW parts company, who had supplied the first one and explained the situation.

"But the alternator's only 13 months old... it can't be that!" he said defensively. *"We supplied it!!"*

"I know! But... if it IS faulty then I need a new one. And I need it in Scotland by tomorrow. Is that possible?"

"Yes, it's possible but not guaranteed. We'll do our best."

"Done!" I said with fingers crossed.

My friend then appeared with the fully charged battery and fitted it in Charlie. I ordered breakfast for us. Charlie was now mobile so we celebrated with bacon sandwiches and more tea.

I then needed to book myself into a campsite in Stirling. The only one that had any space for the next couple of nights closed their gates at 8pm each night. Anyone arriving after eight had to park up for the night on the road. At first, it sounded like I had loads of time to get there, but then I did the maths.

Bloody hell, I was going to need a miracle to make this work...

The ferry was at noon and took three hours. I then needed to drive as far as I could, so I allowed an hour for that. Then approximately one hour wait for a pick-up truck to arrive and load Charlie on the truck. 130 miles could possibly take three hours which got me to... 8pm. Eek!

But, in theory, everything was in place so all I could do was hope. My last call was to the ferry to double check the time of departure.

"Oh, I'm sorry that ferry's fully booked, the next one is tomorrow," was the unexpected answer.

He must have heard my jaw hit the floor and felt the awkward silence of my thoughts going into overdrive when he suggested that I could possibly just turn up in the hope that someone cancelled their ticket. I didn't even bother asking the likelihood of that happening. I just knew I had to get on that ferry.

By then it was 11.30am and I had a 30-minute drive to Port Ellen.

That's a 30-minute drive in a normal car, not Charlie, but luckily the Islay roads were empty and smooth so I just had to pray that nothing got in our way. The final amazing heroic act from my new friend was to escort me to the port, at break-neck speed, and we arrived as the first vehicles were boarding. He waved me on and mouthed *"I'll wait here just in case!!"*

"THANK YOU!!!" I mouthed back, patting my heart.

I parked up to one side waiting for all the ticketed vehicles to take their place and for them to see if there was any space for Charlie.

"Please, please, please, please, please, please, please..." was my mantra as I fixed my gaze on the marshal checking off the vehicles. He finally turned with a thumbs up and beckoned me on to the ferry! Wahoo! I turned to see my friend waving happily in celebration and Charlie tooted back at him. The noise woke Kenny who yawned slowly and curled up, none the wiser.

Miraculously, when I got to Tarbert, Charlie started first time and I looked up to thank the heavens once again. I drove only about 30 minutes to a place called Ardrishaig and parked up in a church carpark sporting a NO PARKING sign. I hoped He wouldn't mind. But it was a town that had Wi-Fi, the road was flat and there was enough space in the carpark for a truck to pick me up.

I waited the expected hour for the breakdown man to arrive and explained that we needed to get to the campsite before 8pm. After a short sharp intake of breath through his teeth, like the ones women get at a garage before the mechanic says *"It's gonna cost you"*, he looked at his watch, exhaled with a bit of a snort but said nothing.

By this time the weather had taken a turn for the worse. It was raining hard. The kind of rain that bounces two feet off the ground and wipes out visibility two feet from the windscreen. But I soon realised what his snort meant. It meant *"OK, I'd drive like a lunatic in any weather to get you to your campsite in time, and let's just pray that we all get there alive."*

After about an hour of this white-knuckle ride, with me looking backwards to see Charlie swaying from side to side, and ergo Kenny, hoping the straps would hold, I had to remind him that his cargo was my whole life so I requested him to slow down. I was happy to camp in the driveway of the campsite if we arrived late. But he didn't really listen so I held on for dear life and prayed.

I sighed the biggest sigh of relief when we arrived, literally as they were shutting the gate. Charlie was still on the back of the truck. I knew there was a restaurant on site so I asked the guy at the campsite if it was still open.

"It's just closing... but tell you what, why don't I unload your van from the truck and park him up while you run to the restaurant to see if you can catch them in time. You're in plot 101."

How lovely of him. So I ran. On hearing my desperate tales of breaking down on an isle on the other side of Scotland, my lunatic breakdown driver, and that I had a cat in the van, which is always a winner to get attention and sympathy, the restaurant kindly re-opened the kitchen and made me some soup with cheese and bread and I guzzled half a bottle of wine and went to bed. How lovely were they too!

•

I got a call in the morning from the mechanic at the Stirling garage saying that the alternator had arrived, ahead of schedule, and that he could fit me in that morning. I can only describe his garage as a classic VW haven. Vintage Beetles and campers everywhere, up on the ramps, being resprayed, new interiors being fitted and engines being pimped. It was awesome! With Charlie (and Kenny) up on the ramps I spent half a day with the mechanic as he combed through Charlie's undercarriage looking for the problem.

Everyone had been right. It wasn't the alternator!

"What's wrong with him then?" I asked, like a concerned parent.

"Well, first of all, it's a miracle that you even got out of London, and a double

miracle that you got this far without breaking down! Someone's looking after you..!"

He then took me on a tour of some of the dodgiest electrics he'd ever seen. Frayed cables hanging on by a thread, cables flapping about going nowhere, cables wired in a most unusual way. And as he talked me through them, he tightened, snipped, re-secured and re-cabled until Charlie was electrically ship-shape and safe.

He checked the old alternator and its wiring, he checked the new throttle cable and the new wiring to the leisure battery. All got a thumbs up!! Phew!

"While you're down there..." I hesitated, *"can you just... check the clutch cable?"*

Luckily I had a spare cable in my tool box. Five minutes later the worn out clutch was replaced just in time! Double phew!

For four hours he spun his mechanical magic. Simultaneously, I got a four-hour intensive mechanics lesson with more oily tea and biscuits. My kind of morning. He photographed Kenny curled up on the back seat saying that his son would never believe him that a cat was in a van up on the ramps and because we'd had such a fun time he decided to only charge me for two hours work. My faith and love for people, especially Scottish ones, just keeps on growing.

I returned to the campsite that night knowing that this was going to be my last night in Scotland. As I ate my last supper in Charlie I felt an aching sadness take over me. I didn't want to believe that my adventure had come to an end. When would I feel this sense of freedom again, this sense of space and utter control of day to day destiny? Not in London, that's for sure.

Once again, I mooted the idea of not going back. What if I just kept going... my *Thelma & Louise* version of events made me laugh out loud to myself as I pictured me holding Kenny's paw as Charlie careered off a cliff. But, seriously, what was I going back to? Life alone with no job. That familiar feeling of *it's me against the world again* returned. Though this time it didn't actually fill me with as much dread as it had in my loneliest hours of my previous life. I now had a sense of fulfilment. I'd done exactly what I had set out to do. I had done something most people will never get the chance to do. I now knew I was courageous, I was tenacious, I was a free spirit and a survivor. I even succumbed to the fact that I might even be a little bit brave! I had let my demons go and let true beauty in. But most of all, I was a loner and proud of it.

This journey had started as a midlife crisis. But after spending 40 days and 40 nights in my van, with my favourite stripy four-legged friend in my little blue house on wheels, I knew that I had undoubtedly had a midlife-affirming, midlife-changing adventure that had changed me for ever.

TWENTY FOUR

9th Aug: Goodbye Scotland

PHOTO REFS P2 – P1

The morning came and the time had come. I took my time tidying the van and having a chat with Kenny. My spot in the campsite had been very secluded and Charlie was backed up against a high dense hedge that led on to a huge cornfield. The corn was taller than I was and I could just about see it swaying in the gentle breeze as I peered through the hedge.

I opened the back of the van to clear out the fridge when Kenny, in slow motion, leapt out of the van, through the hedge and into the cornfield.

"NOOOOOOO! Not now Kenny!!" I shouted in true Inspector Clouseau style that left me staring open-mouthed at the hedge.

I froze to the spot. How on earth was Kenny going to find his way out of a corn field? A couple of turns and he'd be completely lost! How was I meant to find him? If I ventured through the thick hedge and into the cornfield even I'd be completely lost in a couple of turns.

A chilling feeling crept over me that Kenny had gone for ever. What if I never saw him again? The thought numbed me. I called out several times but cats aren't dogs and don't have recall. I shook his food bowl and rattled his jingling scratch post and waited. Nothing. Auto-mode took over and I decided to finish getting the van ready. I had a shower and returned to Charlie pacing around trying to force some practical thoughts together as to what to do next.

Fifteen minutes must have gone by when suddenly *BOUFF...* Kenny hurtled through the hedge, back in to the van at break-neck speed as if he'd seen a ghost! He leapt on to the back seat panting, eye's darting.

What on earth had happened out there! But KENNY!!! YOU'RE HOME!!!
How did you find your way back?! I let out the biggest sigh of relief and
quickly closed all the doors just in case 1) his adventurous spirit had just
been awakened and he was priming himself for his next feat of bravery,
and 2) whatever had startled him in the cornfield was coming after him,
and possibly me.

We had a cuddle and ate breakfast together with the doors locked and
I knew that that was the finale of my Scottish road trip. It was time to go
home.

I don't really remember the drive from Stirling to the English border
but I do remember that the weather had turned grey and it was cold and
raining when I drove past the 'Welcome to England' sign on the M6.
What a perfect welcome back to a now monotoned country.

Blimey, I will miss so many things about Scotland.

I'll miss the silence. The solace. The clarity of thought.

Feeling drunk from the vistas knowing that every day I would be
punch drunk on these very views.

I'll miss being the only person on the road for miles and miles and
miles.

I'll miss the single-track roads, the long winding roads, the long
straight roads, the passing places and blind summits.

Boarding ferries and leaving ports.

The post office, local shop, petrol station combos run by one family.

I'll miss waving to everyone who drives on the Isle of Islay.

The one horse towns.

Living like a nomad. Embracing less is more.

Spending all my time with Kenny.

The freedom of not knowing where I will be from waking in the
morning till parking up at night.

No spreadsheets. No schedules. No pressure.

Meeting genuinely kind people and making new friends.

Having the time to really talk to people.

The beaches. My God, the beaches.

Driving past local breweries and smokeries and popping in for a four-pack of locally brewed ale and dinner.

Cooking and eating al fresco on rocks, beaches and blankets.

Watching Kenny run riot around the van whilst I'm trying to sleep.

Wild camping and washing in waterfalls.

The lack of midges. Where on earth did they all go?

The crazy weather. Scotland certainly knows how to soak you in rain, blow you over in the wind and then produce a sun that burns you, all within 15 minutes.

The whiskies. The gins. The ales.

The fiddles. The whistles. The accordions. The pubs.

Aye, I'll miss Scotland.

This wasn't a holiday, it was a journey.

TWENTY-FIVE

Forty days and forty nights

I'm writing this chapter on the 40th day of isolation in our brave new world and am wondering if I can compare the last forty days, locked in a flat, with my life-changing forty days in the van.

When lockdown was first announced, I thought I'd have this licked. If anyone can hang out on their own for a prolonged period it's me! I live alone, I've travelled on my own, this'll be easy. But, in truth, I found the first couple of weeks really tough. Practically all of my friends were isolated with their families, partners or friends and were posting photos of them together in the garden, having BBQs, drinking cocktails but, most of all, being together. Now don't get me wrong, I'm not saying that's a bad thing for them to be together but, for anyone living alone, the idea of total isolation with no human contact was like a huge ACME hammer to the head saying *"You're not actually going to speak to anyone you know face to face for the unforeseeable future."*

Oh right, this *is* going to be hard...

It brought back all those haunting emotions of being totally forgotten. I could feel that creeping layer of loneliness I thought I'd peeled off starting to engulf me again. I knew I couldn't give in to it so I needed to steel myself and take this on the chin. The one big lesson I had learnt was to be vocal, honest and open with my emotions and to ask for help, so I posted a message on Facebook, and sent it directly to my close friends, that read:

Just a thought... for anyone else like me who is living alone, and is therefore being isolated alone, I have just realised I'm not speaking enough!!

To my lovely friends... if you're about to text me can I ask that you pick up the phone instead so we can chat and laugh out loud.

You know I LOVE to talk so I'll be calling not texting too.

And this is when my friends and acquaintances split like Moses parting the waves. To my delight, some friends shone like beacons of hope, some hidden gems broke free and ran through the abyss to become better friends, whilst, simultaneously, some who I thought were friends crept silently to the other side never to call.

Within a few weeks my social life had never been better. Phones calls, video calls, quiz nights, shared yoga sessions, shared meal times, hangovers and laughter. A revelation. But the most important change was that my friends were calling ME, instead of me feeling needy by calling them. And these were long, meaningful conversations getting to know each other again and hearing stories and sharing ideas that we had never done in our previous incarnation. Long may these connections last.

I also appreciated the advantages of being an introvert. With all this solo time, my batteries had never been so highly charged and this little Duracell bunny was now full of beans and banging her drum. My time was spent baking as many different breads as I could and indulging in the secret recipes released by three of my favourite brands... Warburtons offered up their ingredients to make six crumpets – though I only had a star-shaped biscuit cutter but that made them look all the more special; Wagamama's chicken katsu curry - if I was ever on death row that would be my last supper; and Gregg's steak bake – without doubt, the perfect hangover cure wrapped in puff pastry. My other sources of entertainment were of course Kenny, who continued to be an utter joy and a constant source of out loud laughter; writing, how else do you finish a book; and my bike which was well oiled and well ridden around the ghosted streets of London.

The nation is now entering week seven of isolation and, to be honest,

I like it. I don't want it to go back to the chaos and the lack of care that we were all numbed or enraged by. I know the NHS is at tipping point and that our economy is broken but I think the nation are starting to positively re-wire through acts of kindness. We have already re-evaluated the level of importance that key workers hold in our society, wealth has been shared by some of the elite, and the extraordinary generosity from people during such financially worrying times that tipped £30m for Colonel Tom's constitutionals for the NHS charities. Arise Sir Tom.

I get the feeling that success will no longer to be measured by status nor pay cheque, the fastest car or exotic holiday destinations. It will be measured by one's level of inner happiness and the outcome of finding that without a commercial price tag. People have started to enjoy a quieter life with less pressure, they are valuing precious time spent with their loved ones and will appreciate seeing and hugging their friends again. And finally experiencing a less-polluted environment. Who would ever want to go back to the old normal?

I don't know how long this lockdown is going to go on for but, in some ways, I'm glad that it will go on longer than 42 days. There's magic in the six-week-rule as it takes that long to effect change, effectively. On average, it takes six weeks for broken bones to heal, six weeks to recover completely from surgery, to re-cleanse one's liver, to see and feel the true effects of a healthy diet or exercise. A foetal heartbeat can be detected via ultrasound after six weeks. But above all, a radical six weeks or more of isolation gives everyone the chance to pause, think, percolate and change.

It took me six weeks of driving around Scotland to find, know and love myself again and those feelings are now ingrained. I have learnt and I have changed. I am no longer lonely, I am no longer that bitty person that so many people knew. I am now confidently and enthusiastically looking forward to my wonky path – wherever that may lead.

The four day bolt-on

PHOTO REFS Q1 – R1

Oh yes, how did my forty days and forty nights in the van end…?

After driving past the rainy 'Welcome to England' sign with a heavy heart, it soon lifted as I remembered I had one more isle to go. I picked *Nearer Than Heaven* by Delays as my track of the day as that was one of the promos I'd produced for my Hilbre Island music industry friend who I was about to meet again. It matched my mood as I was already reminiscing about my trip with recurring smiles as I navigated the route he suggested through the undulating beauty of the Lake District, onto the Wirral.

The *plan* was to have a good old catch up, walk out to the island, see one of his famous sunsets, soak up one last beautiful vista, stay for one night and then begin the inevitable journey home. But, as you already know, my plans come with form.

I parked Charlie at the top of the hill and my friend came bounding up to greet me with a huge smile. There's something so comforting in seeing a friend from your past again. We'd always had such a laugh when we'd worked together, I was looking forward to our banter.

I scooped up Kenny and his toys and headed to his house. The first thing I did was sit on the sofa and, with eyes closed and head back, exhaled the biggest "*Aaaahhhh!*" This was the first sofa I had sat on for 40 days and I needed at least 40 seconds to let that feeling of comfort engulf me. My friend sat next to me dying to ask me every detail of my trip but, instead, he just smiled, made me a cup of tea and said "*It's time to decompress.*" And that's exactly what I did. I stayed for four days.

Nine months on...? We haven't stopped talking, laughing, listening, sharing, planning and creating. If I believed in luck, which I don't, I would have hoped to have been lucky enough to *find myself* on my road trip. I certainly wasn't expecting to find my soulmate, best friend and new business partner. To be honest, I think he was as equally surprised but we both know that we've definitely now found each other.

Even though we live 230 miles apart, and lockdown has restricted all physical contact, we have certainly made use of our free mobile minutes and we talk on the phone at least two hours a day – every day! In fact we go for walks together, we watch movies together and he's also taught me how to play the guitar via Zoom. Funny how living remotely can bring you closer together.

We share the same values and vision for the future and, for us, Scotland holds the key. More specifically, Knoydart, the remote peninsula he told me about before I had even set off. We have already set up a company together and have launched a creative retreat for songwriters, photographers and painters called The Knoydart Retreat and are developing other projects that make us spring out of separate beds each morning.

It's curious to think that if I hadn't seen his original message on Facebook, or had just decided not to go on his suggested adventure, then my path would have lead somewhere else and my future would look completely different.

I will always have my adventurous spirit to thank for that,
oh and my future 80-year-old self for giving me
that much needed kick up the arse.

It's a numbers game

▲	B	C	D
2		IT'S A NUMBERS GAME	
3	2,415	Miles driven	London to Scotland and back again
4	155	Miles cycled	see Bike rides
5	40	Days in the van	Biblical
6	40	Nights in the van	
7	14	Live bands	HebCelt, pubs and open mics nights
8	15	New friends made	And still in contact with most
9	9	Boats	Ullapool to Stornoway, LEWIS
10			Tarbert to Uig, SKYE
11			Armadale to Mallaig, MALLAIG
12			Mallaig to Inverie, KNOYDART
13			Kilchoan to Tobermory, MULL
14			Craignure to Oban, OBAN
15			Easdale Island Rib
16			Kennacraig to Port Askaig, ISLAY
17			Port Ellen to Kennacraig, MAINLAND
18	8	Distilleries	Harris
19			Talisker
20			Ardnamurchan
21			Tobermory
22			Oban
23			Ardbeg
24			Lagavulin
25			Bruichladdich
26	8	Isles	Lewis
27			Harris
28			Skye
29			Mull
30			Islay
31			Hilbre
32			Mid-Eye
33			Little-Eye
34	6	Leaping salmon	Rogie Falls
35	6	VW T2 campervans spotted	2 red, 1 beige and 3 yellow
36	5	Bike rides	Bakewell
37			Applecross
38			Harris
39			Skye
40			Islay
41	5	Locally brewed cases of beer	Fyne Ales
42			Skye
43			Knoydart
44			Veterans Brewery
45			Islay
46	5	Midge bites	Little blighters
47	4	Wild camping nights	Applecross, Cliff, Loch Eil
48	4	Days in the Wirral	The bolt-on
49	1	Music festival attended	HebCelt
50	1	Presbyterian church service attended	Stornaway
51	0	Solo travellers on the road in a VW	Only me!
52	0	Camping cats on the road in a VW	Kenny you are unique!

MY SCOTTISH ROUTE

2,471 mile round trip

AND HUGE THANK YOUS TO...

Duncan Lewis for his abundance of support and encouragement, for being the Yang to my Yin and for suggesting I go to Knoydart in the first place. Life would be very different if you hadn't!

Nick Herrmann, my Editor from Cornerstones, whose encouraging words and copious colourful notes made the editing process really enjoyable.

Mandy Martinez, a truly wonderful friend, for proofreading a book written by someone with a U in English Language O'Level. Sorry!!

Danielle Allen, another beautiful friend, and the first to read the final manuscript. Great notes my lovely.

Phil Brisk, an extraordinary work coach, who first planted the seed that I could even write a book.

Auntie Den Hosking for being another enthusiastic beta reader, for letting me live in her flat in Covent Garden to finish the book during lockdown and for taking up the mantle of Auntie Advice Bureau.

Holly McMannus, the British Shorthair Silver Tabby breeder, for bringing Kenny into this world.

Katy and Chris Grazebrook for co-parenting Charlie with me and being my bubble family during lockdown.

John-Boy for being the most fantastic and generous mechanic (I've still got your 'attitude adjuster' by the way!)

Stella Bland for opening my world to the joys of sprouting beans.

Arabella Howell, Spot and Leopard for showing me the ropes on how to travel in a van with cats!

To my sister Sarah de Nordwall whose poetic words of wisdom were most welcome. A true bard.

To my cousin Em for being my rock.

All my family and friends for being so fabulous.

To Belinda Grew for helping me find my first and last job in 'the media'.

My new lovely friends I met on the road especially Shelagh & Pete, @catscannondales & @wheel-skills and Lorri & her lassies.

And finally to everyone who went over and above the call of duty to help me out when Charlie broke down including Mike Meakin, Tom Hunter and his whole family, Andrew Macdonald and Donald Harvey.

QR CODE FOR SPOTIFY

Hold your phone camera over the QR code
to open soundtrack in Spotify

The Stone Roses	*Waterfall*
America	*A Horse With No Name*
Crowes Pastures	*Slow It Down*
Ludovico Einaudi	*Fuori Dal Mondo*
The Undertones	*Teenage Kicks*
The Chameleons	*Swamp Thing*
Johnny Nash	*I Can See Clearly Now*
Gillian Welsh	*Orphan Girl*
Creedence Clearwater Revival	*Bad Moon Rising*
The Innocence Mission	*Edelweiss*
Eurythmics	*Sweet Dreams Are Made Of This*
Talking Heads	*Road To Nowhere*
Delays	*Nearer Than Heaven*

ABOUT THE AUTHOR

I'm more surprised than anyone that I wrote a book. Some people say there is a book in everyone and I have always disagreed. But then I embarked on a six-week road trip and here I am writing a paragraph, at the end of my book, about the author!

Since leaving my full-time job last year I have thoroughly enjoyed developing creative projects about things that I really care about. Long may that last.

Kenny still makes me laugh every day and Charlie still tootles.

www.janeydenordwall.com   www.theknoydartretreat.com

 @silverjaney   @knoydartretreat

@silverjaney67